M000247596

Musings on Internal Quality Audits

Having a Greater Impact

Also available from ASQ Quality Press:

Performance Metrics: The Levers for Process Management
Duke Okes

Root Cause Analysis: The Core of Problem Solving and Corrective Action
Duke Okes

Advanced Quality Auditing: An Auditor's Review of Risk Management, Lean Improvement, and Data Analysis
Lance B. Coleman

The Internal Auditing Pocket Guide, Second Edition
J.P. Russell

Quality Audits for Improved Performance, Third Edition
Dennis R. Arter

The Quality Toolbox, Second Edition
Nancy R. Tague

The Certified Six Sigma Green Belt Handbook, Second Edition
Roderick A. Munro, Govindarajan Ramu, and Daniel J. Zrymiak

The Certified Manager of Quality/Organizational Excellence Handbook, Fourth Edition
Russell T. Westcott, editor

The Certified Six Sigma Black Belt Handbook, Second Edition
T.M. Kubiak and Donald W. Benbow

The ASQ Auditing Handbook, Fourth Edition
J.P. Russell, editor

The ASQ Quality Improvement Pocket Guide: Basic History, Concepts, Tools, and Relationships
Grace L. Duffy, editor

To request a complimentary catalog of ASQ Quality Press publications, call 800-248-1946, or visit our Web site at http://qualitypress.asq.org.

Musings on Internal Quality Audits

Having a Greater Impact

Duke Okes

ASQ Quality Press
Milwaukee, Wisconsin

American Society for Quality, Quality Press, Milwaukee, WI 53203
© 2017 by ASQ
All rights reserved. Published 2016.
Printed in the United States of America.

22   21   20   19   18   17   16   5   4   3   2   1

Names: Okes, Duke, 1949- author.
Title: Musings on internal quality audits : having a greater impact / by Duke
    Okes.
Description: Milwaukee, WI : ASQ Quality Press, [2017] | Includes index.
Identifiers: LCCN 2017018303 | ISBN 9780873899581 (alk. paper)
Subjects: LCSH: Auditing. | Auditing, Internal. | Auditors' reports.
Classification: LCC HF5667 .O44 2017 | DDC 658.4/013--dc23
LC record available at https://lccn.loc.gov/2017018303

No part of this book may be reproduced in any form or by any means, electronic,
mechanical, photocopying, recording, or otherwise, without the prior written
permission of the publisher.

Director, Quality Press and Programs: Ray Zielke
Managing Editor: Paul Daniel O'Mara
Sr. Creative Services Specialist: Randy L. Benson

ASQ Mission: The American Society for Quality advances individual,
organizational, and community excellence worldwide through learning, quality
improvement, and knowledge exchange.

Attention Bookstores, Wholesalers, Schools, and Corporations: ASQ Quality
Press books, video, audio, and software are available at quantity discounts with
bulk purchases for business, educational, or instructional use. For information,
please contact ASQ Quality Press at 800-248-1946, or write to ASQ Quality Press,
P.O. Box 3005, Milwaukee, WI 53201-3005.

To place orders or to request ASQ membership information, call 800-248-1946.
Visit our Web site at www.asq.org / quality-press.

 Printed on acid-free paper

Quality Press
600 N. Plankinton Ave.
Milwaukee, WI 53203-2914
E-mail: authors@asq.org

ASQ   **The Global Voice of Quality®**

Dedication

In memory of Russell T. Westcott

Contents

List of Figures and Tables

Preface

Many books on quality auditing are already available, so why take the time to write another? Well, for over 20 years I've spoken and published articles on the topic and trained an estimated two thousand internal quality auditors as well as a few folks wanting to become ASQ Certified Quality Auditors. However, while most internal quality audits perhaps meet the basic needs of the organization, I believe much more could be done to add higher value.

I had the good luck to perform my first audit in a country where I didn't speak the primary language and where the organization was a startup (not yet operating) that did not yet have a formal quality system in place. So all I could do is rely on the principles and practices of auditing, an international quality management system standard, and an interpreter to guide my efforts. All went well, and I ended up working with the organization to close the gaps.

Auditing is basically a component of process management, intended to determine whether the desired controls have been effectively implemented (the Check in the Plan-Do-Check-Act cycle). They provide a feedback mechanism, hopefully, an early warning, that allows modification of business processes before negative outcomes impact organizational objectives and stakeholders.

This book is a compilation of some training materials I've used, talks I've given, and articles I've published. It is not intended as an introduction for new auditors, but instead is intended for those who understand the basics and are looking for ideas for how to improve what their organization gets out of the internal quality audit process. While some of the ideas may be less viable in certain industries (especially those that are highly regulated), it is my hope that the ideas will at least expand the view of what is possible.

The book is broken into three parts. Section 1 is a summary of the basic quality audit and intentionally does not include things such as training of auditors, basic auditor competencies, and so on. However, it does look at some of the more recent changes in the audit process driven by changes in standards, technology, and globalism. Section 2 includes several concepts and methods that organizations can choose to use if they want to make their quality audits more robust from a standpoint of achieving the intended purpose. Section 3 then intentionally pushes back from the standard perspective of auditing as a technical process for control and looks at softer issues that an audit program might leverage. It also tries to project a bit into the future as to how the audit role/process might change.

Some qualifications:

1. While this book is focused on internal audits (first-party audits), it is likely that many of the ideas are also relevant for external auditing, whether it is of suppliers or third parties.

2. Standard audit terminology (for example, as in ISO 19011) uses the sequence of "Preparing for" and "Performing an audit." In my training, speaking, and writing I have consistently used the simpler terms *Plan* and *Conduct* and will continue to do so in this book.

3. Throughout the book when mentioning aspects of a quality management system (QMS), the ISO 9001 standard will be used as a general description of requirements. However, the principles and practices discussed would likely be just as applicable if an organization is not using ISO standards.

My thanks to the many organizations, groups, and individuals who have given me opportunities to share my ideas over the years. Examples include the ASQ Auditing and Quality Management Divisions, Rocky Mountain Quality Conference, Toronto Quality Forum, numerous local ASQ sections, and Paton Press's *The Auditor* (now owned by Exemplar Global). Thanks also to Richard H. Gregory, who did some of the early cleanup of the old texts, and to Lance Coleman for helping me flesh out some of the ideas for the risk-based auditing material.

As always, the author would love feedback, especially anything you find that helped add greater value to your organization or additional techniques you've implemented that really made a difference.

Section 1

Basics and Current Conversations

The Fundamentals

1
Basic Audit Principles and Practices

WHY CONDUCT INTERNAL QUALITY AUDITS?

Simply put, when an activity or process is carried out, we can either wait until it is complete and see if the results are acceptable, or we can monitor the process while it is operating and detect variances that might cause unacceptable outcomes. Which would you rather have: a state trooper who writes a ticket for your speeding, or your own active monitoring of your speedometer (a self-audit to determine how well your controls are working) as you drive so you can make necessary adjustments to stay within the speed limit?

Audits are intended to identify potential problems with process controls before they cause problems. Of course, an audit can also be done retrospectively after a problem has resulted in order to identify causes. In this case, it is part of the data collection process for performing root cause analysis.

Quality audits usually are conducted by measuring compliance to requirements, such as quality management system standards, customer contracts, regulatory requirements, and internal policies and procedures. Audits can also be conducted using other frameworks or guidelines that allow detecting opportunities for improvement in the design of an organization's processes. Since compliance is not the primary purpose in this case, they are sometimes termed assessments.

Organizations have multiple management systems in place, each intended to satisfy and/or protect specific stakeholders. For example:

- A quality management system (QMS) is intended to protect the customer

- A safety management system (OHS) is intended to protect employees

- An environmental management system (EMS) is intended to protect the community/society within which the business operates

- The financial management system is intended to protect owners/investors

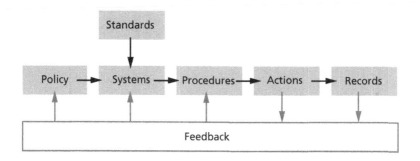

Figure 1.1 Audits as feedback.

In essence, auditing is one aspect (performance metrics are another) of the Check portion of the Shewhart Plan-Do-Check-Act cycle for developing, deploying, monitoring, and improving a process. Figure 1.1 is an example of the flow of requirements into activities and results, and the role of audits for providing feedback.

Internal audits are carried out by auditors working at the bequest of the client, who is usually senior leadership or the process owner of the organization, facility, or process being audited. Any problems found are reported as nonconformities, which may mean that processes do not meet the requirements of the customer, external standards to which the quality system is aligned, or internal policies and procedures. Nonconformities are often ranked as major or minor, depending on the degree of risk. Other observations during the audit that are not clear nonconformities, but instead represent a potential concern or opportunity for improvement, can also be reported.

Audits can also be carried out with different levels of focus:

- System audit—Looks at the entire quality management system, or a major portion of it, in order to determine if high-level policies and procedures meet requirements and if those requirements have been effectively implemented.

- Process audit—Looks at one or more specific processes in depth in order to determine whether the inputs, resources, controls, and outputs meet requirements. These are often conducted on higher-risk processes. Note: The term *process audit* should not be confused with audits conducted using a "process approach."

- Product audit—Evaluates samples of the product, whether in-process or completed, to determine whether they meet requirements at that point in the process flow.

Combinations of these three types of audits can, of course, be done if deemed useful. For example, a product sample might be evaluated during a process audit.

PLANNING AN AUDIT

Audits typically are not done *ad hoc*, unless there are indications of a system breakdown that someone would like investigated. Instead, they are carried out according to a pre-established, typically annual audit schedule. When an audit is to occur, the audit manager must identify the purpose (why is the audit being done) and scope (what portion of the quality system and/or organization should be audited), as well as the auditors who will carry out the audit.

Simply, the purpose is often to carry out an audit according to the audit schedule, although special audits may be requested. The scope is also typically predefined as part of the audit schedule. Selecting auditors requires consideration of auditor qualifications, independence of the area to be audited, and their availability.

The auditors then must develop an audit plan considering issues such as:

- What standards, policies, procedures, and other documents should be reviewed prior to the audit? See Table 1.1 for examples of the types of documents that might be reviewed.

- How much time is available for the audit and how will work be divided among the auditors if there are more than one?

- Will key personnel be available on the audit dates?

Table 1.1 Examples of documents reviewed for audit planning.

- External quality management system standards (e.g., ISO 9001)
- Quality manual and/or procedures
- Regulations, contractual requirements, specifications and organizational objectives
- Work instructions/SOPs
- Forms or databases used to record results
- Results of previous audits
- Critical product and/or process parameters
- Resource requirements (e.g., materials, equipment, information, number of personnel)
- Personnel competency requirements

The auditor(s) should then develop checklists that define what will be sampled, as well as the sample size and technique(s) to be used to evaluate the samples. Typically this will be a mix of interviews of personnel in the process, observation of people and/or equipment as they carry out relevant activities, and/or reviews of process records. If an organization uses pre-established checklists, it is useful for auditors to first review them and the associated policies and procedures so that the audit doesn't simply become a "checking off" process. Audit checklists play two important functions: 1) guiding auditors so they remain in-scope, and 2) providing space for documenting findings.

Experienced auditors often have less need for checklists and may simply have a copy of the relevant standards, policies, and procedures with them during the audit. In advance of the audit, they can identify areas of most interest, but can be less constrained during the audit. Findings can also be written on the documents. Of course, the use of tablet computers, iPads, and so on makes this even easier, with audit reports being nearly automated.

Prior to conducting the audit, the auditors should notify managers/supervisors of the areas to be audited, clarifying the purpose and scope of the audit and names of auditors who will carry out the audit, as well as the dates/times to be spent in each area to be audited. This should be done sufficiently in advance so that it will not disrupt the work areas.

Confirmation by those who oversee the areas to be audited should be obtained. This allows management of the areas to be better prepared to provide personnel to answer auditor questions, facilitate access to needed processes and information, and provide working locations for the auditors when necessary.

CONDUCTING THE AUDIT

The formal audit process requires that an opening meeting be held between auditors and management. However, once an internal audit program has been running successfully for a period of time, this step may add little value. However, if an opening meeting is done, basically it should just reiterate the notification information, confirming that it is still acceptable to go forward. A record should be kept of attendees. Sometimes audit schedules can be sidelined by the absence of key personnel, equipment that is down, surprise visits by customers or regulators, or other things that call for a temporary shift in priorities.

The audit itself then consists of collecting data. Each of the three data collection methods has its own strengths and weaknesses, and a good auditor will often collect information about the same issue using more than one method in order to establish greater confidence in the resulting conclusions.

The interview process consists of putting people at ease, getting answers to questions, thanking auditee(s), and then exiting the area. Some general recommendations are that auditors:

- Not ask leading questions (for example, where the correct answer is implied)
- Not be argumentative, but must probe as necessary to gain the required information
- Actively listen and indicate they are doing so (for example, perhaps by nodding)
- Occasionally summarize, in their own language, what they understand the auditee(s) to have stated
- Use silence appropriately
- Not "hide" nonconformities until the closing meeting

When possible, observing processes in operation should be done without interference. Also, remember that the observer impacts the process, so auditors often need to observe multiple cycles (for example, different parts, orders, people) to evaluate consistency. Special attention should be paid to what happens when there are problems with the product/ process. For example, is there an appropriate response?

Reviewing records involves verifying that the correct recording form is being used, all required fields are filled in with the right information, the record is being produced in a timely manner, and the information indicates that the process is satisfying requirements (for example, process controls, product characteristics). Again, if requirements were not met, was appropriate action taken?

Auditors also need to be aware of, and able to deal with:

- Resistance to the perceived "authority" role of an auditor
- Attempts by auditees to divert from the topic
- Fear, uncertainty, and/or conflicts among auditees
- Efforts to challenge the system
- Misunderstandings by the auditor

Examples of real human situations encountered during past audits by the author:

- *During an ISO 9001 preassessment, the quality manager could not be found. Eventually, it was determined he had locked himself in the ladies' room in order to avoid being audited.*

- *In another preassessment, a product engineer continually avoided providing answers to specific questions about the design process. The engineer's manager was informed that the audit could not be completed.*

- *During a gap assessment, the knees of one individual were observed shaking (ok, the author has occasionally been said to resemble Chuck Norris, but hopefully his questions didn't feel like karate!). This particular interview was terminated early, then completed after the individual had the opportunity to hear from others how it had gone for them.*

Auditors must remain focused during the audit by thinking how the process is supposed to work (for example, according to documented procedures), and by collecting sufficient evidence to confirm compliance (or lack of it) and trends. The auditor needs to maintain a written record of findings, with specific details for any nonconformities found. The details might include the title of person audited, document number, part number, or other references, and where and when the nonconformity was found. When two or more auditors are working as an audit team, they should occasionally stop for audit team reviews, compare findings, make adjustments to the audit plan if necessary, and write nonconformities.

Auditors must also be flexible and adapt to special situations that arise. For example, an auditor who observes a potential safety problem should immediately notify someone in a management role. An auditor may also need to adapt to other changes in the work environment, such as a process suddenly shutting down or resources being redeployed. And if, during the audit, there are indications of quality process problems that fall outside the scope of the audit, the auditor must decide whether or not to modify the audit plan to investigate the new trail.

An auditor can make two types of errors regarding nonconformities. A type 1 error is interpreting something as a nonconformity that really is not, and a type 2 is not interpreting something as a nonconformity that really is (see Figure 1.2). Each has the potential to cause harm, and auditors must drive to make decisions objectively, that is, based on facts.

Existence of a Nonconformity?	Is a Nonconformity Reported?	
	YES	NO
YES	Desired	**Type 2 Error** Undesired
NONE	**Type 1 Error** Unacceptable	Desired

Note: The terms Unacceptable and Undesired might be swapped if the entity is a very high-risk environment where failures must be avoided.

Figure 1.2 Types of audit errors.

Examples of responding to special situations encountered by the author during past audits:

- *During an audit, an inside corner of the building was observed to have a tarp hanging from the ceiling, indicating that perhaps something was being shielded. When the auditor asked what it was, he was told it was a proprietary piece of equipment. This caused the auditor to raise a question as to whether it was part of the scope of their quality system, and if so, whether it should be included as part of the audit.*

- *When being escorted from the office area into the plant, the auditor and escort had to step around a puddle of water in the aisle. The auditor asked whether it might be advised to put a barrier around the puddle to ensure that someone didn't step into it and slip and fall.*

- *As the auditor was walking toward the purchasing manager's office, the manager stepped into the hallway and stated he had just been requested to meet with the general manager. This then required a shuffle of the audit schedule for that day.*

- *The auditor was reviewing product drawings and noticed that all samples pulled had the letters "REV" on them, but no one had entered a revision number in the space beside it. Luckily, rather than relying on past experience to interpret the findings, the auditor explored it further. It turned out that the individual who reviewed and approved drawings had the initials REV!*

REPORTING AUDIT RESULTS

When the auditors have collected and analyzed the data, it is time to report their findings formally. For a formal audit process, this is done via both a closing meeting and a written report. As with opening meetings, a closing meeting may not be that useful if an organization has been conducting internal audits for a long time. However, if audits are infrequent, which means they likely cover a large portion of the system, then the closing meeting may add value.

If a closing meeting is held, it should look something like this from an auditor perspective:

- Record the names (and perhaps titles) of all attendees
- Restate the purpose and scope of audit, and clarify the "sampling" role of auditing
- Present any positive findings—things believed to be outstanding
- Present nonconformities verbally (and in writing if specified by the audit procedure) and be prepared to support them with objective evidence

- Present any other observations or concerns
- Answer questions about findings

If auditors have done their job well, the audit meeting will be brief and concise. It is very important to avoid giving advice on how to correct any deficiencies, since the auditors are not in a system management role during an audit and typically do not have ownership of the processes audited. This does not mean the managers can't ask for ideas later when the formal auditor is in their normal functional role.

The audit report should be issued shortly after the audit and follow a standard reporting format that will typically include:

- The audit purpose and scope
- Audit date(s) and number (if used)
- Audited departments, processes, and/or QMS elements
- Standards or other referenced used
- Findings (nonconformities, observations)

The audit report then includes a formal request for corrective action for each nonconformity that warrants action.

CLOSING THE AUDIT

The final step in the audit process is closing the audit after all corrective actions have been addressed. This requires that someone follow up to determine whether corrective actions were taken and whether or not they were effective. Sometimes this is done by the same auditors who identified the nonconformities, and sometimes by other auditors as part of a later regularly scheduled audit.

See Appendix A for examples of situations used for discussion during auditor training to help consider different ways of responding.

2

Recent Evolution in Audits

While the overall audit intent and process hasn't changed dramatically, changes in standards and technology have caused quality (and other) audits to evolve somewhat. Some examples include an emphasis on conducting audits based on a "process approach," conducting integrated audits, conducting virtual audits, more service organizations using ISO 9001, and fewer procedures and paper records. Each calls for changes in perspectives and/or skills in order to gain the potential respective advantages.

AUDITS BASED ON A PROCESS APPROACH

An audit can be organized many different ways:

- **By department**—An audit of this type would focus primarily on the activities carried out by a particular functional group, such as purchasing or testing. Many different requirements could be assessed (see Figure 2.1). This type of audit might be especially useful if recent performance of the organization has been significantly impacted by the processes carried out by a specific department, or if the work group is at a remote location relative to the rest of the organization.

- **By requirement**—As shown in Figure 2.1, most QMS requirements impact many different functions and processes, and an audit that assesses this specific requirement in depth could be carried out. Again, if recent performance of this requirement has been bad, and/or there have been changes to either the requirements or how the organization carries out the related processes, an assessment of that requirement across the organization might be warranted.

- **By order flow**—Sometimes called a "trace audit," this type of audit follows one or more transactions from order receipt from the customer through the order fulfillment process until the order is complete (product or service has been delivered to the customer). Along the way, multiple other system requirements can be assessed at each step of the flow (for example, competencies of people, availability of adequate physical resources), allowing a good cross sampling to occur. It also allows seeing whether interconnections or handoffs between workgroups are effective. Of course, the audit can also be done in reverse, from order delivery back through operations into order receipt. Partial audits can simply start and end anywhere along the flow path.

Quality System Element X=Primary Authority/Responsibility O=Involvement in Process	President	Sales Manager	Engineering Manager	Materials Manager	Production Manager	Quality Manager	Human Resource Manager	Controller	Maintenance Supervisor	Lab Supervisor
			Department Manager							
Quality Management System Design & Documentation	O	O	O	O	O	X	O	O		
Management Planning & Performance Reviews	X	O	O	O	O	O	O	O		
Provision of Physical Resources	X	O	O	O	O	O	O	O		
Human Competencies	O	O	O	O	O	O	X			
Planning of Operational Processes		O	X	O	O	O	O	O		
Customer-Related Process		X	O	O	O	O				
Product Design Control			X	O	O	O				
Purchasing			O	X	O	O			O	O
Operations		O	O	O	X	O			O	O
Calibration of Monitoring/ Measuring Devices			O		O	O			X	O
Performance Measurement & Monitoring		O	O	O	O	X	O	O	O	X
Nonconforming Product Control		O	O	O	X	O				O
Corrective Action & Improvement	X	O	O	O	O	O	O	O		

Figure 2.1 Matrix of QMS elements and departments.

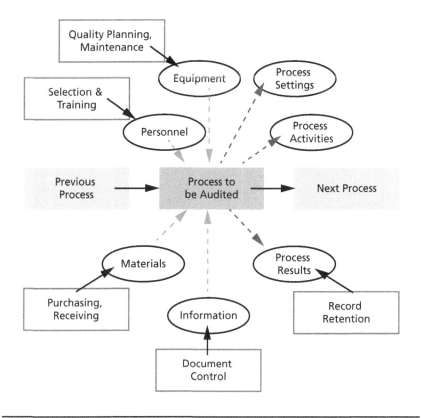

Figure 2.2 Interrelationship of QMS processes.

The latter is similar to using a process approach, in that when assessing a particular step of the process, one can look at the inputs, activities, outputs, knowledge/status of personnel and/or equipment, performance against objectives, and so on (see Figure 2.2). The other aspect of the process approach is using the Plan-Do-Check-Act cycle during the audit. What are the relevant plans (policies, procedures, instructions, and so on), are they being implemented, how are process personnel verifying results, and what do they do when results are not satisfactory? Note that this can be done at the micro level (one specific activity or step in a process), a midi level (an entire process) or a macro level (the entire QMS). By default, if one is auditing the entire system, then the process approach is being used since the ISO standard itself is designed based on PDCA.

However, while the process approach is currently being emphasized in the quality audit community, it is not inherently better than the other options. Granted, it is more efficient for an auditor from outside the facility who wants to audit all or a significant portion of the system in a single visit. But for local auditors, who often conduct smaller audits more frequently, design of the audit should take into account the current needs of the organization.

Another way of looking at it depends on what one means by "process." For example, document control is itself a process, with inputs (needs for specific documents), outputs (the document, whether paper or electronic) available to personnel who need it, and activities (drafting, reviewing, approving, distributing). So if a particular element of the QMS system is of major concern, seeing and auditing it as a process is appropriate.

Another factor is the pace of each of the interrelated processes. For example, calibration may be carried out monthly for hundreds of devices, while training of metrology personnel is likely to be done much less frequently. So while auditing the calibration process, one might pay a lot of attention during each audit as to whether devices were calibrated at the appropriate time, level of accuracy, and so on, but looking at the competency of calibration personnel each time may not make much sense unless there has been turnover of personnel or new types of devices have been introduced into the calibration system.

An advantage of the process approach (which really should be called a process view) is that it reinforces the need for organizations to effectively design, execute, monitor, and improve processes. Another advantage is that the results of one process are often significantly impacted by other processes. This has been emphasized in each update of the ISO 9001 standard, as well as other management system standards.

Auditing using a process approach requires having a more complete understanding of all QMS requirements and flexibility in audit path. That is, within any process, many different process interfaces could be audited, and the breadth and depth of the audit along each path carefully selected and planned in order to keep the audit focused and efficient.

The turtle diagram (similar to Figure 2.2) is often used by auditors to help plan an audit. The author prefers to use a SIPOC analysis form, as it is a more standard practice for process management thinking. See Appendix B for an example.

INTEGRATED AUDITS

Although some organizations have conducted internal quality system audits for decades, for many it was a new function driven by implementation of a QMS based on ISO 9001 or one of its industry derivatives (for example, automotive and IATF 16949, medical devices and ISO 13485, aerospace and AS9100, telecom and TL 9000). Then along came an environmental management system standard (ISO 14000) and more recently an occupational health and safety standard (ISO 45000). Each requires internal audits.

Organizations often found themselves conducting multiple audits, each focusing on a particular type of management system. But all the standards also had requirements for policies, for controlling documentation, for training, for internal audit, for corrective action, and so on, and auditors recognized the potential for performing audits of multiple systems simultaneously. This is, of course, aided if the systems themselves are integrated (for example, same document control and/or competency management processes are used for all).

Integrated audits require that at least some members of the audit team be knowledgeable of multiple management systems in order to gain the efficiency of integration. However, one factor that complicates this occurs when the processes being audited have the intent of implementing legal and regulatory requirements, violations of which can potential result in a major fine or jail sentence (the same is true for QMS audits in some industries). The competency of auditors as well as how audit findings are reported then becomes even more critical.

Integrated audits certainly provide a more comprehensive view of the adequacy of controls overall, since they replicate how the business is operated. That is, we integrate quality, safety, environmental, and other activities into each work process where relevant. Planning for such an audit is then more likely to benefit by having a flowchart of the processes to be audited, with relevant controls identified. Ranking of the importance (for example, degree of risk) of each control could also be included.

Integrated audits are likely to be more and more emphasized in the future, as standards for information security (ISO 27000), energy management (ISO 50000), and others are developed and implemented. However, there will always also be the need for specialists in each type of system who understand the depth and nuances.

VIRTUAL AUDITS

Many changes have led to the use of virtual audits, such as more global organizations spanning geographic boundaries, increasing costs and frustration with air travel, and virtual access to nearly anywhere in the world through the Internet. While on-site audits may be critical in some situations, the use of virtual audits, also called e-auditing or remote audits, can often allow greater coverage at lower cost.

The technologies that enable virtual audits include Skype, Webex, and other such platforms, e-mail and text that allows human-to-human interface and documentation transfer/review, cameras that can allow a virtual tour of the audited facility, and the ability to provide auditors with access to the organization's ERP or other computerized document management systems (such as those used for change control, corrective action, training records, and so on). Obviously, security, fraud, and other concerns are heightened by some of these changes. And communication skills become even more important since there are more likely to be cultural, language, and other such issues that auditors must be aware of and adapt to.

Such audits can be done synchronously or asynchronously, as is much of the day-to-day work in today's organizations. However, due to the trust necessary for effective audits as well as the experience of auditors with face-to-face audits, virtual audits have been slow to become common. It is, of course, somewhat easier for internal audits where both parties are from the same organization.

It is highly unlikely that virtual audits would be used for initial audits of an organization where the relationship has not previously been established. However, even in such cases, access to electronic documents could be made available in advance to allow the onsite audit to focus on higher risk and/or more difficult areas to audit. Follow-up audits might then be done remotely.

It is also advisable to provide training and/or written procedures to auditors who will conduct virtual audits. This might include what situations are or are not acceptable for virtual audits, as well as standards for how access should be gained and documented. In some cases, additional training might also be necessary for software and equipment involved in the audit process on either end.

While virtual audits are often touted as a way to reduce costs (airfare, hotels, rental cars, meals), it is the impact on auditor productivity that should be the primary interest. An auditor who spends a day getting to the audit site, followed by a three-day audit, then another day returning home, is only able to audit 60 percent of the time. By eliminating the travel, a larger proportion of auditor time can be spent on the actual audit process.

This section brought up an interesting question: What role might drones play in future audits?

AUDITING PROCESSES WITH LIMITED DOCUMENTATION

Some organizations, process owners, and other individuals find documented procedures to be bureaucratic or constraining, and ISO 9001 has indicated for some time that the degree of documentation may depend on the complexity of the process and/or knowledge of the individuals involved. In fact, each revision of the standard has typically reduced the number of required procedures to where the latest edition provides a lot of flexibility.

However, auditors have traditionally relied on documented procedures as the primary baseline for planning an audit and process records as their primary source of objective evidence. This means that if one is auditing a process that has little or no documentation, other methods must be used for determining both requirements and results. Following are some options:

- **Use the ISO standard itself.** Not only does the standard specify the minimum processes required, but also details of some of the controls those processes must include.

- **Talk to the process owner.** Whoever is ultimately responsible for the process should be able to describe the specific inputs, resources, activities, controls, and objectives. This individual might be a manager, an engineer, or anyone responsible for designing the organization's processes within a functional area. What this individual specifies during an audit interview can then become the process requirements to which the assessment can be done.

- **Speak with the trainer.** For some processes, there will be specified trainers who developed the curriculum and/or are responsible for conducting the training for personnel in the process. Their lesson plans, handouts, and tests can be used to develop guidelines for assessing the process.

- **Speak with those who perform the process.** They should be able to describe the process requirements (for example, inputs, outputs, activities, controls) and why they are important. Interviewing more than one individual who carries out the same process can then help identify whether the process is being managed consistently.

- **Examine the process objectives.** The purpose of organizational and process objectives is to establish performance metrics that allow the organization to predict how well customer and stakeholder requirements will be met. Auditors can first study the objectives, then ask what activities are necessary to achieve them. They can also determine the degree to which metrics indicate unstable or incapable performance, and how consistently responses to performance problems are managed.

- **Get feedback from the customer or other process stakeholders.** Who knows best whether the process is working as it should? The individuals/processes that receive the output! Starting with the customer to determine the requirements and how well they are being met, then working back into the process to see how it is being managed, is a fundamental process management audit.

Auditing a well-documented process may be easier, but it can encourage auditors to rely too narrowly on that documentation and not see the bigger picture. Understanding good process management practices, such

---

Good Process Management Practices

The quality management principles that were used for guiding development of ISO 9001 provide a framework for understanding good process management practices. Following are four such principles, along with typical components of each, which could be used for developing auditor questions, regardless of whether or not there is any documentation to audit.

Customer Focus—Every process has one or more customers. Individuals within each process should know who their customers are, the customer's expectations, what activities must be carried out in order to meet those expectations, and how well the expectations are being met.

Leadership—Every process (regardless of level of the organization) has an individual, the process owner, who is responsible for the process. That individual should ensure that customer requirements are known and communicated, policies and processes are defined that will fulfill the requirements, adequate resources (equipment, people, information) are available in order for the processes to be carried out appropriately, and objectives and metrics are used to evaluate outcomes and/or to control the process.

Involvement of People—Everyone in the organization should be aware of overall organizational policies and objectives as well as those of their department and/or work group. They should work with process owners to align day-to-day activities with policies and objectives, and communicate any problems that retard the ability to achieve them. They should set and achieve individual objectives that continually improve their contributions to the objectives.

Process Approach—Every activity in the organization should be seen as a part of a process that has customers who specify output requirements. In order to meet those requirements, adequate resources, activities, and controls must be designed and implemented, which includes working with external or internal suppliers who provide the necessary inputs. Objectives and metrics for monitoring, controlling, and improving performance of the process are in place and continually used for feedback on the design and execution of the process.

Figure 2.3 Process management principles.

as those listed in Figure 2.3, will allow auditors to examine nearly any process, regardless of available documentation. Of course, more care may be needed to triangulate or validate findings when documentation is not available, but following good process management practices will provide a better view of system performance.

AUDITING SERVICE PROCESSES

A major shift in processes that are likely to be audited has occurred. At one time the focus was on manufacturing and distribution processes that involved physical processes and products having quantifiable and physical outcomes and characteristics. This is no longer true as globalization, technology, and demographic shifts have resulted in a multitude of service-oriented processes that are subject to audit.

Such processes typically produce tangible but not necessarily physical outputs. They are also susceptible to more inherent variation due to the greater degree of human interaction, exposure to the randomness of the outside world, and service provider/customer interaction.

The ISO 9001 Auditing Practices Group guidance on auditing service organizations discusses the need to assess how the service is designed and validated, and how nonconformities are dealt with. Although performing these processes will help ensure the development of a robust process and ways of dealing with failures, it is the actual delivery process that customers see and that therefore shapes their perceptions of the organization.

Outcome-focused information for service applications that don't produce easily measured results should be assessed almost immediately after the interaction, using open-ended questions such as "What was really good about the experience?" and "What could have been done better?," as well as determining whether basic contractual, departmental, or customer obligations were met. A series of output user satisfaction surveys (whether internal user, another department, or retail customer) conducted over a period of time can allow trend analysis but are less likely to tap into the immediate emotional experience unless they are conducted immediately after or concurrently with initial use.

Direct observation, audio recording, or reviewing security videos can work well with service organizations interacting with the public. For example, some service organizations hire mystery shoppers who purchase their services and then score how well the interaction occurred based on criteria established by the organization. This allows the introduction of various scenarios to see how well the system responds. In effect, the mystery shoppers are auditing the process.

Anonymous peer reviews is another option wherever there's an opportunity for a knowledgeable but disinterested third party to observe and record interactions between the provider and customer/user. However, such evaluations may need to be more principle-based than activity-based since expectations for some aspects of the service may not be clearly established in advance and may need to change as the situation progresses,

In principle, auditing a service-oriented process is no different from any other auditing activity. It calls for trained auditors, standards against which the audit will be conducted, and collecting and reporting information that describes how well the process is working. However, service data are likely to contain more sources of noise, since high verbal interactions between customer/user and provider must take into account differences in values, priorities, moods, and expectations and can, therefore, cause wider variation in perceived results. This is perhaps more so in consumer services than business services, where professional codes of conduct and/or the more structured environment may somewhat constrain behaviors.

AUDITING DIGITAL PROCESSES

Many business processes are now carried out by digital computers that provide a highly automated process that eliminates transfers of physical documents between individuals and departments. An example is an enterprise resource planning (ERP) system that automatically screens incoming orders (received via electronic data interchange/EDI) and schedules them, places orders with suppliers for the resources necessary for order fulfillment, then generates shipping notifications and invoices to customers once the order has been shipped.

Such levels of automation have been around for a long time in the accounting arena, but the widespread application of systems such as SAP has significantly increased the number of quality audits that will encounter such digitalization. In quality management, environmental management, and occupational health and safety management (QMS, EMS, OHS), the use of software to manage the workflow for processes such as change control and corrective action also increases such opportunities.

The strength of these digitalized processes is that they automate the mathematics, storage, and communication of mass amounts of data, and also, in many cases, decision-making processes formerly done by individuals and/or groups. It's also their weakness because the results of these automated processes are not readily visible at every step of the process, and, if they are available, are likely to be in machine-readable form. Additionally, the processes are likely to span people and organizations at different geographic locations (think about Amazon.com). The combination of these factors means that the usual audit techniques (interviews, observation, and reviewing records) aren't suitable for the audit task, and can't provide a high degree of assurance that the processes are performing as they should.

So what to do? Well, just as we would want to know that a human was trained correctly, we need to know that the computer system was designed and implemented correctly. This can be done by looking at the system inputs and outputs, the flow of logic between them, and the decision criteria and rules (procedures) for each step of the process. For many systems, this will have been documented as part of system design and development, and auditors can review this information. However, it is important to note that software documentation is notoriously the weak spot since the software is constantly changing, upgrades and bug fixes become a permanent feature, and platforms are constantly changing.

Confirmation that the process performs correctly should have been done as part of system testing and validation. Auditors can look at both the processes for and the results of that validation. But, the auditor must take extreme care to make sure that the documentation used reflects the current configuration. Note that validation should look for both type 1 (in which a "no" decision is where a "yes" should be) and type 2 (a "yes" decision where a "no" should be) errors. Control of revisions to the system should also be confirmed, along with proper access security for administrators, programmers, and users.

Further confirmation can be done by accessing digital files (records) to verify that the system still operates according to the criteria, although in many cases information technology (IT) personnel may need to translate the data into human-readable form. It's interesting that in the financial controls audit arena a technique known as "continuous auditing" is sometimes used to automatically assess transactions (and in parallel with the normal processing of those transactions) for patterns that might indicate problems such as errors or fraud. Such techniques are likely to be expanded in the future for analyzing a broader range of processes.

It's important that auditors of digital management processes be familiar with basic IT hardware and software terminology, as they may need to interface with IT personnel during such audits. IT personnel will also have to arrange for appropriate temporary system access for auditors where needed to perform the audit. It's also important that the auditors are confident that the system/process they're auditing is stable, "virus" free, and that no one can manipulate it during the audit period. Auditors will also need to be familiar with the appropriate modules of the respective systems to be audited.

One advantage of digital systems is that auditors don't necessarily need to be on site during the entire audit. Downloads of system files or electronic access through a remote portal can allow auditors to spend time reviewing system design documents or transaction records in detail regardless of the auditor's location.

However, as the ISO 9001 Auditing Practices Group indicated in an August 2005 guidance document on auditing electronics-based management systems, auditors should not rely solely on remote access, but should also confirm the existence of physical processes/resources supported by the computer. Globalization will obviously require a conscious effort by auditors to balance the issues of cost vs. effectiveness.

An interesting thought: one day auditors will be interviewing intelligent robots. Artificial intelligence embedded in customer service interfaces, for example, automated phone systems, verbal order entry portals, and others.

Section 2

Ensuring Rigor and Governance

Going Deeper

3

Auditing in Depth

Auditing for depth can mean many different things. In this book, it means to think about the particular portion of the QMS being audited, and to dig down into more detail than would typically be done during a system audit that tries to assess a large portion of the system and/or organization.

AUDITING SPREADSHEETS

Spreadsheets are widely used throughout organizations as part of controlling and monitoring processes. Maybe it's a pricing spreadsheet used by Sales, or a measurement system analysis spreadsheet used by Quality. The question to ask is which of them deal with information that could impact quality? For those that can impact quality, how robust was the process for creating and validating it? How well are any revisions controlled? Who has access to them?

A key salesperson in one organization maintained a spreadsheet documenting pricing strategies and their application to each customer. When the individual retired, the next salesperson was not aware that a price reduction included in the document for some customers was to be in place only temporarily. Unfortunately, it was applied for a considerable amount of time beyond the temporary limit before someone discovered the resulting revenue shortfall.

The point is that spreadsheets are very powerful tools, but they are often under the control of a single individual. Some common examples include:

- Supplier rating systems

- Cost of quality reports

- Gage R&R studies

- Sales pricing formulae for quoting contracts

- Engineering design calculations

- Scheduling capacity estimation
- Performance scorecards
- Web analytics
- Testing trend analyses

So what should auditors do? When auditing they should be on the lookout for spreadsheets that are part of the quality management system, either directly or indirectly. What are they used for and how are they controlled? Give special focus to those user-generated spreadsheets involving calculations. When failures in these decisions could be related to performance problems the organization has previously encountered, dig deeper to see if the spreadsheet has contributed bad information.

What should you look for when auditing spreadsheets? Here are a few considerations:

- Who created the spreadsheet? Is it an appropriate tool for the application? Why did they feel the need to create it? Should it be integrated into a more formal IT system?
- Is cut/paste used? How are formulae and macros protected from accidental modification by users?
- How was the spreadsheet validated and is it under change control?
- Is the spreadsheet included as part of the document control and/ or records management practices as appropriate?

There are many examples of how small errors in data have created major problems (remember loss of the Mars orbiter due to a contractor's use of English measurement units in a command, instead of metric as specified in the NASA contract?). Inadequate control of spreadsheets provides many opportunities for such issues, and should therefore be considered for inclusion in any audit. At a minimum, there should be an occasional inventory of spreadsheets to determine which ones need to be controlled from a quality/risk perspective.

AUDITING X-Y CORRELATION

The whole point of an audit is to ensure that the controls necessary for achieving objectives are in place and being properly applied. So let's think of the objectives as Y and the controls as the $X's$ that will affect whether Y turns out as desired.

Audits often only deal with $X's$, and not whether their performance is actually correlated with Y. And their relationship can be looked at as having four possible combinations (see Figure 3.1). Auditors often make assumptions

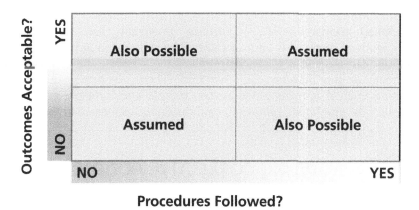

Figure 3.1 Potential relationships between controls and outcomes.

that if the procedure is followed, the outcome will be acceptable, and if the procedure isn't followed, the outcome will not be acceptable.

However, note there are two other combinations that indicate the potential for a more in-depth audit process:

- The procedures were followed (the controls are in place), but results weren't as expected. This might indicate that the variables are not related in a meaningful way, that there are other factors unaccounted for in the controls, or the data are perhaps flawed in some way.

- Procedures weren't followed (controls were not working), but results were as desired. This might also indicate that the procedure has little influence over the results; that is, the process is robust enough to produce acceptable results even if the controls are not followed properly. This may mean there are opportunities to reduce controls (and their related costs).

When evaluating the correlation between controls and outcomes, an auditor must take care to relate the output set (Y) to its source activity (X) from a time orientation. For example, running a process on day one might not yield results until day three. That would be the case if, for example, packing and shipping was audited. Results wouldn't come in until the recipients opened their packages.

Whether controls or outcomes are considered first depends on the circumstances. Looking at outcomes first presupposes that controls information for that outcome set is available and can be evaluated. However, if the controls must be observed in real time to get an accurate assessment, then the outcome evaluation must wait until the time when its performance is measured.

In summary, *X-Y* correlation is a powerful mindset for auditors if applied properly, since it is more powerful than independent investigations of controls and outcomes. Not only can it aid in detecting controls variances, but it can help determine whether the controls are adequate or are perhaps even wasteful. There are opportunities for learning even if it turns out that the controls and outcome evaluated together are unrelated. The auditor might ask questions such as, "What was it that led the organization to assume a correlation?"

AUDITING CORRECTIVE ACTION

Unfortunately, closing out corrective action requests in a timely manner is a metric often used for evaluating the performance of the process. Obviously, a better metric would be to determine how often the same problem recurs. However, if one understands root cause analysis and corrective action in depth, many other issues not dealt with in the standards should be considered when auditing the corrective action process:

- **What factors are used to determine which problems require corrective action?** In some cases, organizations pass over opportunities for driving improvement through the corrective action process, but more frequently they overload the process by throwing every problem into it. A screening process for evaluating problems based on factors such as frequency, related risks and cost, and perhaps also availability of resources and opportunity costs should exist.

- **Was the depth of the investigation appropriate and was a conscious decision made to go to that depth?** There is often a lack of understanding of the difference between the physical cause and a system (root) cause, with many corrective actions focusing only on the former. This is entirely appropriate assuming the decision is based on proper rationale, but the rationale cannot exist if the organization does not differentiate between the two types of causes. In effect, the corrective action process needs to include a conscious choice as to the appropriate depth of the investigation.

- **Was appropriate logic and evidence used to find the cause(s) of the problem?** Finding the physical and system causes of problems requires a combination of deductive and inductive thinking (the interaction of theories/hypotheses and evidence), which is not typically taught either in schools or in organizations. Most corrective action procedures also do not contain guidance on how to do the investigative process. A lack of such guidance leaves investigators with little choice but to do what they believe is appropriate, with the resulting poor performance of the investigations.

- **Is there proper alignment of solutions to cause(s)?** If one assumes the cause(s) of the problem were correctly identified, that does not mean the actions taken are necessarily appropriate for resolving the causes. Instead, what may have been done is simply a temporary patch, or in many cases something that actually makes the process less efficient and increases costs (for example, adding another check step). Or maybe there's no relationship between the solution and the cause!

- **Is the process owner appropriately involved in the investigation and solution implementation?** In many organizations, the quality group is asked to perform the investigations. It must then impose solutions on processes over which it has no direct day-to-day implementation control. While it may make sense to have individuals with such backgrounds involved in the investigation, it is critical from an ownership standpoint to have the process owner heavily involved (if not guiding) the investigation.

- **Are unintended consequences considered when solutions are selected?** When one changes a system in order to solve one problem, it is quite possible that the change will have other effects. Consideration of these potential effects should be done prior to implementation, with appropriate modification of the solution or monitoring for the effect.

- **Is the culture of the organization one that supports effective root cause investigations?** In high-performing organizations, problems are seen as learning opportunities, while in poor performing ones they are often seen as indicating the need for discipline. In the latter case, individuals will not be open and honest, which means the evidence required for an effective investigation will not be available. The net effect is a poor investigation, resulting in repeated occurrences of the problem.

Remember that the Act stage of PDCA occurs when the system self-corrects. When the corrective action process doesn't work well, there will be no significant learning. This process calls for a deep level of analysis when it is being audited.

AUDITING LEVELS OF PROBLEM PREVENTION

ISO 9001 stipulates controls such as document approval, products/process validation, personnel competencies, and equipment calibration/maintenance as ways to reduce the probability of failures during operations. The idea is to ensure that processes will meet objectives.

Problem prevention action can occur at different stages of a process:

- **Before the fact.** This is one of the purposes of the risk-based thinking requirements of ISO 9001 (formerly called preventive action). If, when we're developing a new product or process, we consider what could go wrong, we might identify opportunities to prevent some of them by redesigning the product/process in some way. So if we find a nonconformity during an audit, we should go back and see if that problem had been predicted during the development process, and if so, what decisions were made that allowed it to still occur. It may have been that the risk was accepted, the failure rate inaccurately estimated, or the controls put in place were not well designed.

- **During operations.** As a product/process is being operated, measurements will usually be available that let us know how well it is working. If we see a drift in performance that might eventually cause a problem, we can take proactive action to counteract it. Auditors then should not just look for nonconformities, but trends in performance, whether or not the trends have been identified by process owners, and what decisions, if any, have been made on how to respond to the trend. Keep in mind that the trends could also be positive, indicating an opportunity to be seized.

- **After the fact (during corrective action).** When the organization has conducted a root cause analysis and implemented a solution to prevent the problem from recurring, it should also consider where else in the organization those specific problems and/or causes might occur. In some cases, the same solution can be put in place. Auditors should determine whether or not this scanning process has taken place, and what decisions were made as a result.

Regardless of the circumstances, assessment of any problem or potential problem should first evaluate the related risks and opportunities, and make a conscious choice as to whether or not to respond. Auditors should ensure that evaluating this decision process is part of process management during planning, execution, and corrective action.

AUDITING FOR SUPPLY CHAIN RELIABILITY

The globalization of the supply chain has brought many opportunities for firms to reduce costs and better focus on their core competencies. However, it also brings related risks. Audits of potential suppliers are often done in order to assess that risk but they do not necessarily consider all the factors that can create supply chain risk. If an organization is going to audit suppliers, some fundamental questions they should ask include:

1. **Who should and should not be audited?** While a company might rate its suppliers as A, B, and C based on the volume of business and/or how integral the product/service is to the company, it does not indicate anything about the supplier's potential reliability. If, however, other customers, regulatory bodies, and so on have information on how well an organization performs, then an audit may not add significant value. In a nutshell, companies for which information is not readily available should be audited if they play a key role in the success of the organization who wants to do business with them. In addition, it may not be just the direct supplier, but in fact a supplier to that supplier who should be audited (remember the supply chain is only as strong as its weakest link; see Figure 3.2, where the refrigerator company may be put at most risk if the tool and die manufacturer fails).

2. **What should be audited?** Traditionally the quality system was the major focus of supplier audits (along with credit status checks by purchasing or accounting). The objective of the audit was assurance that the supplier could operate consistently within agreed-to limits, which decreased the risk of product quality problems. However, that audit process, by focusing on the supplier's product process, didn't address the larger picture of risks the supplier faced nor how effectively the supplier's processes dealt with them. Table 3.1 provides examples of different situations and some of the items that might be assessed during an audit in order to evaluate potential risks. The list could easily be expanded to look at other important business processes such as development and execution of strategy, post-delivery support, public relations, and continual improvement methods/successes.

3. **Who should conduct the audit?** The answer to this question is easy after question #2 is answered since auditors must be knowledgeable of the processes they will audit. The audit team may then be led by a generalist, working with specialists from scheduling, HR, IT, and so on (see Figure 3.3), as is often done for an integrated audit. The audit team might also consist of multiple partners in the supply chain.

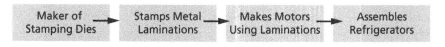

Figure 3.2 Partial supply chain.

Table 3.1 Items to evaluate considering potential supplier situations.

Situation	What to Assess
The supplier operates near production capacity limits, or has unique equipment in the value creation process	Equipment reliability, business expansion plans, scheduling system
The supplier is highly regulated and would be shut down by a significant violation	Records of compliance to appropriate systems (e.g., safety, environnmetal) and how well the system adapts to changes in the organization
The supplier is highly impacted by the performance of its suppliers	% of resources allocated to supplier management, record of past performance of the firm's suppliers
The supplier has high employee turnover or is a cyclical business	Employee selection methods and training practices
The supplier is highly financially leveraged	Cash management practices, relationships with financial backers, likely future financial demands
The supplier heavily utilizes unique information technologies for critical applications	How IT system reliability is maintained

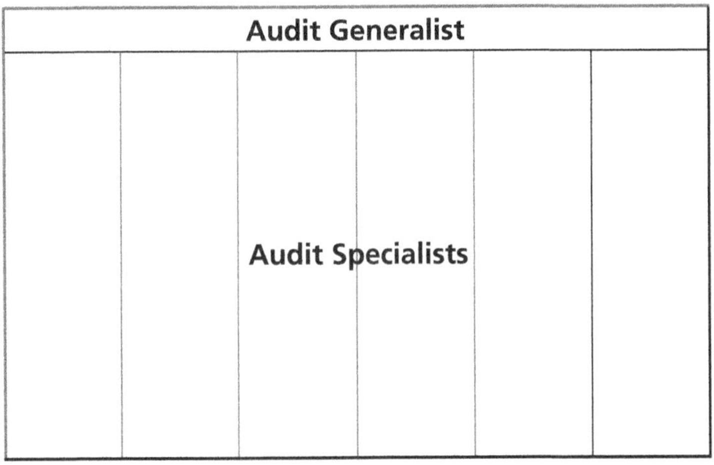

Figure 3.3 Makeup of a supplier audit team.

The key point is that the likelihood of a supplier being audited depends on its role in the supply chain, and uniqueness and importance of its role. Rather than assessing all possible suppliers, employ the Pareto principle to select the key suppliers based on risk. The auditors should then assess the selected suppliers' compliance systems and the performance of their systems over time. This will require that the auditors be given access to the supplier's historical records, and will constitute a major test of the supplier's openness and willingness to be a good and effective supply chain partner.

In essence, if the question "why do we audit our suppliers?" is thought about in depth, then which suppliers to audit and what to audit will flow from the answers. Once the "what" is established, then the "who" becomes clear. Hint: the wrong answer to the "why" question is "because our procedures say so!"

CONSIDERING PROCESS MATURITY

Think about shopping around for a house, but you're just driving around and looking in windows, not doing the inside tour. How many windows do you want to look through for each house? Probably more than one, since what you see through one will be at least somewhat, if not wholly different, than others.

In the same way, a QMS can be viewed from different perspectives. In this case, it's the maturity of the organization's QMS, since as it gets more mature some of the performance frameworks and measures in its early stages will be of less value, and higher-level issues should be considered. Figure 3.4 provides four potential views.

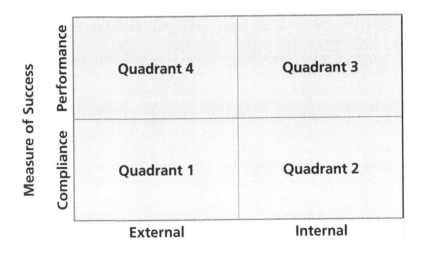

Figure 3.4 Maturity of a QMS.

- **Quadrant 1:** *Assessing External Compliance.* For a new QMS, this is obviously the place to start. The audit will focus on how well the system is designed to comply with external requirements such as ISO standards, specific customer specifications, regulatory body requirements, and so on. For a heavily documented system (for example, lots of procedures), this compliance can be determined by a desk audit that compares the process designs relative to the external requirements.

- **Quadrant 2:** *Assessing Internal Compliance.* When it is known that the system is properly designed, then compliance of personnel to its internal policies and procedures is warranted. This helps determine how well the system has been communicated, implemented, and maintained.

- **Quadrant 3:** *Assessing System Performance against Expectations.* Once compliance has been established and sufficient time has elapsed, the degree to which the system actually achieves desired objectives can be evaluated. Much of the data likely already exists in performance metrics, audit findings, management reviews, and so on, but the independent view of an audit can often detect variances that others have accepted, overlooked, or avoided recognizing.

- **Quadrant 4:** *Assessing Against Benchmarks.* Even though processes and the QMS routinely meet their objectives doesn't mean there aren't still significant opportunities. This can be done by comparing processes and results to external benchmark data, whether it be other facilities within the company, other companies in the industry, or known benchmark companies (such as Baldrige, Shingo, and other prize winners).

A key point is that each process and QMS may be at a different point on its maturity curve. If a QMS performs well in Quadrant 1, then it is mature enough to move on to Quadrant 2, and so on. Planning of audits should then consider the degree of maturity, with appropriate information used as an input for evaluation during the audit. Each process or related audit inquiry can then be flagged in the audit plan to identify where it fits in the maturity matrix.

Somewhere in this matrix, an audit program might also introduce information on competitive intelligence, if available. What are some features of a competitor's QMS and how do they help leverage strategy? However, this doesn't mean the same features should be adopted by the company, since, if the strategy is different, it may call for a differently featured QMS.

ASSESSING AND AUDITING THE AUDIT PROCESS

Sectors such as aerospace (AS9100) and automotive (IATF 16949) have always had different schemes for approval of auditors who carried out the registration process, and also specify additional requirements for internal auditor qualification. One can understand this based on the regulatory and product risk environments.

Given that the QMS in general is about managing risk, it is also incumbent on other organizations to consider raising the bar for internal quality auditors. While involvement of people across the organization has made the audit process more socially acceptable, if the skills and resulting depth of the audits do not produce significant results, then management will understandably be skeptical. So continuous improvement of audits, and therefore auditors, is needed.

As of the date of writing this book, the standard for auditing management systems, ISO 19011, is being updated. Auditor competencies is certain to be a key topic under discussion. Likewise, the Institute of Internal Auditors recently released a new edition of the International Standards for the Professional Practice of Internal Auditing, which includes references to specific requirements for financial auditors.

However, it's unlikely that most organizations utilize ISO 19011 as a requirement for their audit process and auditors since it is not a requirement. But one could easily make the case that there will be a greater need to consider it going forward. Granted, the internal audit program is audited by the external registrar for registered companies, but they are auditing it compared to the basic audit requirements in the QMS standard, not deeper audit requirements.

One way to improve the design of any process is, of course, to get feedback on its performance. For audits this feedback might include:

- Inputs from auditees, process owners, and senior management of the organization on their perception of the audit program

- Looking at the number of findings by external auditors in areas that had been recently audited by internal auditors

- Looking at system weaknesses, identified by root cause analysis, when doing corrective action for quality failures, which had not been identified through the audit program

A starting point for more independent assessment of an internal quality audit program could be to have it reviewed by the organization's internal financial auditors, who typically have much deeper audit experience. Benchmarking audit programs from medical device or pharmaceutical companies might be useful for improving basic risk control audits. Either/ both of these would likely help identify potential changes to the audit program so that future audits would look at issues in more depth.

4

Effective Audit Reporting

A udit reporting is somewhat related to marketing. Auditors have planned and conducted the audit, but now it's time to present the findings. How well the organization responds will be impacted by how well the auditor packages and presents the results. In addition, visibility of the overall audit process can impact whether or not people view it as added value or just a perfunctory duty.

ARE NCS NUISANCES OR PROBLEMS?

In a way, the answer to the question depends on your perspective. Think of it this way: a nonconformity (NC) in a process could be nothing more than a minor nuisance from the organization's perspective because of the relative risks to performance. That's one reason audit reporting the right way is so important.

Also, remember that when people are presented with audit results, they're likely busy with their daily routine—preparing for meetings, writing reports, handling emergencies, and/or attending to personnel matters. They're not really interested in being told that something is wrong, particularly if they view that something as minor. And if it's a major problem they may immediately get defensive because it happened on their watch.

So auditors can learn from highly regulated or high-risk industries that routinely use risk management. They accept audits as a normal part of their business routine. Their familiarity and acceptance lead to an expectation that the audits will be in depth and will generate specific information such as when the problem began, failure rates, trend analysis and, in some cases, even the failure mode.

This means that the audit report should primarily present what prompted the audit, the scope of the audit, and any problems found. Additionally, it might also include the sample size and time frame, which may include reviewing findings from previous audits, in order to determine whether it is a one-off or repetitive issue, and the related risks such as to objectives, customers, regulations, and so on.

Two ways of demonstrating the relative importance of a finding are a risk matrix (see Figure 4.1) and a NC Ranking Table (see Table 4.1). Both of these are typical techniques used in a formal risk management program, something that senior management is likely quite familiar with. At a minimum, audit NCs should be reported not only as how they relate to requirements (for example, of standards, policies or procedures) but also which specific business and/or quality objectives they put at risk.

Always keep in mind that finding a nonconformance is not enough. Neither is classifying it as major or minor, a binary process that often creates a perception of a somewhat arbitrary decision. Presenting it in a way that helps differentiate levels of response can help ensure that it will be believed and handled properly.

Another consideration is whether the singular NCs should somehow be aggregated so as to see the total risk. If, for example, if two NCs each increase the risk of an unsatisfied customer, how much has the total risk to that objective been increased? A more systemic view might also be done by looking at potential interactions of multiple NCs.

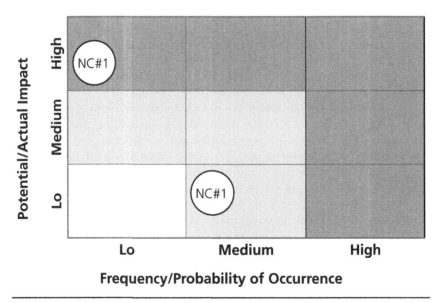

Figure 4.1 Nonconformity risk matrix.

Table 4.1 Nonconformity ranking.

NC Classification	Criteria
Critical	Severe impact on COQ and/or operations, extreme impact on customers/stakeholders
Major	High impact on COQ and/or operations, negative impact to customers/stakeholders
Moderate	Slight impact on COQ and/or operations, unlikely impact on customers/stakeholders
Minor	No measurable impact on COQ, operations, or customers/stakeholders
COQ – Cost of Quality	

INTERNAL AUDIT SCORECARDS

The Information Age has given us advantages and capabilities undreamed of only a few years ago, but it's also given everyone a massive information overload. One way to help people quickly understand performance information is to employ visual aids.

Quality audit program managers are likely to use metrics that help them evaluate the program itself. Such measures might include:

- Number of auditors and their levels of qualification (for example, co-auditor only, audit alone, lead auditor)
- Percent of active auditors (defined as having participated in at least one of the last x audits)
- Number of audits requested
- Percent of audits conducted on time
- Number of nonconformities per audit person-hour or day
- Number or percent of audits done on time
- Number of nonconformances by department, process, element
- Number of audit person-days, number done within budget
- Cycle time to report and close audit
- Number of nonconformances disagreed with, number of observations acted on
- Coverage of audit universe, percent of controls audited

While this information may be value to the auditors, of more value to the organization is a way to see how well each QMS element, process, or department performs overall. An audit dashboard is a graphic that demonstrates performance of the QMS from the audit perspective.

Quality System Element ^ is Good/Green, ~ is Ok/Yellow, ? Is Bad/Red	Department Manager									
	President	Sales Manager	Engineering Manager	Materials Manager	Production Manager	Quality Manager	Human Resource Manager	Controller	Maintenance Supervisor	Lab Supervisor
Quality Management System Design & Documentation	^	^	^	^	^	^	^	^		
Management Planning & Performance Reviews	~	^	^	^	^	^	?	^		
Provision of Physical Resources	^	^	^	~	^	^	^	^		
Human Competencies	^	^	^	^	^	^	?			
Planning of Operational Processes		^	^	^	^	^		^		
Customer-Related Process		^	^	^	^	^				
Product Design Control		^	^	^	^	^				
Purchasing		^	^	~	^	^			^	^
Operations		^	^	^	^	^			^	^
Calibration of Monitoring/ Measuring Devices		^	^	^	^	^			?	^
Performance Measurement & Monitoring		^	^	~	^	^	?	^	?	^
Nonconforming Product Control		^	^	^	^	^				^
Corrective Action & Improvement	^	^	^	^	^	^	?	^		

Figure 4.2 Audit scorecard by element and department.

Figure 4.2 is one format. It demonstrates how well each department has performed according to each of the relevant elements/process of the QMS. Note that it allows quickly seeing which departments and/or elements have had the most serious issues, with a caret (^) indicating no NCs, a tilde (~) indicating minor issues, and a question mark (?) demonstrating serious NCs. If the figure were in color, green, yellow, and red, respectively, would be used for each cell.

Figure 4.3 shows another way to display the information in a way that's more appropriate for process thinking, though admittedly requiring a bit of effort to fully appreciate, as the diagram indicates the flow of processes within the quality management system. Again, performance of each process could be shown by coding each process green, yellow, or red.

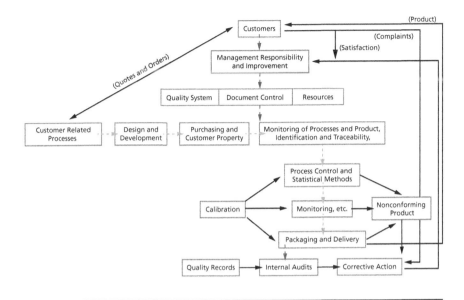

Figure 4.3 Audit scorecard by QMS process.

Either of these two formats could also be adapted to show not only the current status, but also how it compares to the previous status. A time frame for each status window would need to be specified (for example, it is only the most recent audit compared to the one before it, or this year compared to last, and so on).

A BETTER METRIC FOR EVALUATING INTERNAL QUALITY AUDIT

As stated in the previous section, often many metrics are used to track an internal audit program. However, they are primarily efficiency focused, rather than effectiveness focused. What would be beneficial is to have some metrics that can demonstrate the value the audit program brings to the organization. After all, the resources involved in conducting audits might be more valuable if applied elsewhere, so it is important for the audit program manager to be able to demonstrate value.

In order to do so, it is necessary to be explicit about the purpose of the audit process, and that is to prevent system control failures by identifying nonconformances so they can be corrected before outcome failures occur. It is necessary to know how many successful audit events there were and how many failure events, using the following definitions:

- *Success* means that an audit detected a NC that would have led to a quality failure (for example, customer complaint, nonconforming material, process downtime, and so on), and thereby prevented it

- *Failure* means that one of these quality failures actually occurred and no audit detected the control failure that allowed it

Using these definitions the following can then be calculated:

- For each audit NC found, quantify the potential cost of the likely quality failure and the estimated probability it would have actually occurred. This was a successful/effective audit and we can calculate the impact as the cost x occurrence. If, for example, a customer complaint would have resulted in a cost of $20k and we believe there is a 50 percent chance it would have occurred, the success impact is $20k x .5, or +$10k.

- For each quality failure that occurs, quantify the cost of failure and the probability an audit could have detected the control failure, and thereby prevent the quality failure. This is a failure of the audit program, and the failure value can be calculated as the cost of the quality failure x the probability of detection. If, for example, there was a product failure that cost $50k and the probability of detection is estimated at 10 percent, then the failure impact is $50k x .1, or -$5k.

By doing this for several NCs and quality failures over a period of time, the total impact can be calculated:

- Total $ Successes = $\Sigma(\$ \times O)$ for all audit NCs
- Total $ Failures = $\Sigma(\$ \times D)$ for all product/process failures
- Total Impact of the Audit Process = Total $ Successes – Total $ Failures

What does the total impact indicate?

- If it is a High+, then the QMS is "bad" but the audit process is working well at identifying the weaknesses

- If it is a High-, then QMS is "bad" and the audit process is *not* working well

- If the impact is low (for example, near zero, whether positive or negative), then the audit process should be improved. That improvement could include:

  o Improve detection by using better audit process techniques if Total $ Failures is high (increase Value)

  o Reduce the cost of the audit process if Total $ Failure is low (increase Value)

So by finding the impact, it is known how effective the audit process is. But this doesn't take into account the resources used to deliver this performance. So now it is necessary to calculate the value, which is defined as Effectiveness/Efficiency, or the impact of the audit process divided by the cost of operating the audit function.

The value can range from high+ thru 0 to high-. If it is a high+, the organization is getting value from the audit process (but needs to work on the QMS). If value is a high-, the audit process needs to be redesigned. If the value is near zero, there are opportunities to reduce the cost of the audit process.

This is not likely to be an ongoing measurement process, but could be used to get a snapshot in time to evaluate effectiveness and value of the audit process. This information could be used to prove the value being provided or to justify increasing the audit function. However, adjusting audit resources when Total $ Failure is low may be moot in highly-regulated, high-risk industries and/or processes, where audits are mandated and/or high impact, low frequency failures are of too high a risk.

Note that this same concept could be used to look at effectiveness of the corrective action process (for example, the success or failure of prevention of recurrence), and the value of that process. But if the audit process isn't effective, the corrective action process can't fix the system deficiencies before the quality failures occur since they aren't being identified as NCs.

IMPORTANCE OF LANGUAGE

A keynote speaker at an audit conference spoke about how senior management had never paid much attention to results of quality audits, but when the audit program manager started communicating findings in terms of risk, things turned dramatically. No change occured in the audit process itself; just a change in how the information was communicated.

Recent changes in QMS standards will help in this regard, by introducing the language of risk. However, there are other opportunities to use language as a way to better show alignment of the quality audit process to business priorities:

- Use the language of "controls" when talking about actions required by the QMS. Actions such as training, calibration, and supplier performance monitoring are done in order to reduce the likelihood of failure of business systems. In management-speak, such actions are called "internal controls." (For more on this concept, do some light research on the COSO Internal Control Framework for public companies, or OMC Circular A-123 for government entities.)

- Ensure that all communications regarding audits, especially NCs, are tied to specific business objectives. Rather than simply stating the requirement and the violation found, be specific about which top-level business objectives a control failure has the potential to impact.

- Alignment of control failures to specific enterprise risk management categories of risk can also be useful. While most QMS controls are likely operational risks, some may also be strategic, financial reporting, compliance, or other categories used by the organization to categorize risks.

VISIBILITY OF AUDIT REPORTING

How transparent should the organization be with audit findings? Certainly it must be transparent to owners of the processes audited. But how about internal customers of those processes, or suppliers to those processes? How about external customers and/or suppliers? Regulatory bodies? There isn't a single answer to the question, but the question should be considered.

This doesn't mean the entire audit report is widely distributed, but instead it means asking how useful would some of the information be to some of these parties. Would it help them gain more confidence in their relationships? Would it cause them to offer to help in areas that might benefit them?

Remember that there are different types of management system processes being audited, and one can choose which to share more widely. First, there are the core processes (such as contracting, design, purchasing, production), then the support processes (such as resources, training, and calibration), and finally there are the system management processes (such as document control, internal audit, management review). Each has different stakeholders and degrees of inherent risk.

As mentioned in the section on scorecards, reporting should also include, where useful, not only the results of the audit just completed, but also previous audits in the area. Including other performance information (for example, trends in relevant customer complaints and/or other performance objectives) could also help process personnel understand the importance of the findings. Reporting of NCs should also be sufficiently parsed to help identify trends (for example, rather than simply stating the procedure or standard element, indicate the deepest possible sub-clause/paragraph, and so on).

5

Using Risk as a Framework

Just as safety policies and procedures are designed to protect employees, the quality management system is designed to protect customers. Each management system typically has a champion or owner who provides guidance on the external standards or guidelines (ISO 9001 or its derivatives for the QMS), and each requires audits in order to monitor how well the system is working.

However, not every process within a management system has the same level of importance, depending on the organizational context and objectives. It is, therefore, useful to apply the Pareto principle when allocating audit resources. A risk perspective helps guide this allocation.

RISK-BASED QUALITY AUDITING

Financial auditors have done risk-based audits at least the since passing of the Sarbanes-Oxley (SOX) act of 2002. SOX is intended to safeguard the adequacy of management controls for ensuring that financial reports are accurate, and was driven by the fraud perpetrated by Enron, WorldCom, and others. Unfortunately, the auditors were evidently simply checking the boxes and collecting their paychecks.

Quality auditors can learn from this and begin using a formal risk-based orientation to drive their QMS audits. There has certainly been no dearth of major quality failures (think dog food, peanut butter, tires, ignition switches, airbags…).

In general, risk is defined as the combination of the probability of occurrence of an event and the severity of the resulting harm. The risks can come about due to either internal or externally factors, but regardless of the factors, the controls of the organization should be designed to deal with them if deemed too high.

For QMS auditors this means evaluating the risks intended to be controlled, or that might be introduced, by quality-related processes. Ranking the processes based on risk can then help identify which are more important to audit at a higher frequency and/or greater depth.

Figure 5.1 Risk-based audit considerations.

ISO 9001 for some time has indicated that risk should be considered in the audit program; for example, by stating that internal audit plans should consider the "importance of activities" when developing audit plans. Here's what ISO 9001:2015 section 9.2.2 for internal quality audits says the organization shall do:

a) plan, establish, implement and maintain an audit program including the frequency, methods, responsibilities, planning requirements and reporting, which *shall take into consideration the quality objectives, the importance of the processes concerned, changes in the organization, and the results of previous audits;*

This means that organizations should set the frequencies of audits, audit sample size, and depth and direction of audit traces based on:

- A proactive stance that: 1) considers the relevant importance of each QMS process, 2) considers the potential impact of changes to the QMS or the organization

- A reactive stance that: 3) takes into account system feedback such as results of previous audits, customer feedback, and performance metrics that indicate how well the organization is doing relative to quality objectives

These two stances are demonstrated in Figure 5.1. The details of each of these considerations are organized into three approaches for planning and conducting audits.

Approach #1—Consider the Relevant Importance of Each QMS Process

Let's assess the potential risks related to nonconformities (NCs) for some elements of the ISO 9001 standard. In order to do so, the NCs need to be related to risks, which in this case will be the quality objectives. A simple

| QMS Process | Types of Risk | | | | | | | | | | | |
| | Product Function | | | Delivery Performance | | | Regulatory Compliance | | | Cost of Quality | | |
	Probability	Impact	Risk	Probability	Impact	Risk	Probability	Impact	Risk	Probability	Impact	Risk
Customer contracting/ordering	3	1	3	2	5	10	1	4	4	1	3	3
Product design	2	5	10	1	2	2	2	5	10	2	5	10
Process design	2	4	8	2	3	6	1	3	3	2	5	10
Purchasing	3	3	9	4	4	16	1	3	3	3	4	12
Order fulfillment	4	5	20	3	5	15	2	4	8	4	5	20
Calibration	1	4	4	1	1	1	1	1	1	1	2	2
Nonconforming material	2	4	8	2	3	6	1	4	4	2	4	8
Document control	3	4	12	2	2	4	2	2	4	2	2	4
Internal audit	3	3	9	3	1	3	1	2	2	1	2	2

Figure 5.2 Assessment of risk for QMS processes.

preliminary risk analysis can accomplish this, and consists of a list of QMS processes and an assessment of the relative degree of risk of each against achieving the quality objectives. See Figure 5.2 for an example, which uses a scale of 1 (low) to 5 (high) for both probability and impact. The risk score is then the multiple of these two numbers.

The number can be aggregated across and down to determine which QMS elements create the higher and lower risk potentials (looking at total risk across), and which types of risks are more prevalent (summing total risk for each type). These can impact both how the audit process is carried out, as well as how the QMS might be redesigned.

Based on this example risk assessment, the organization would likely audit the product design and order fulfillment processes more frequently than the calibration and process design processes. This would, of course, be unique to a specific product/service type and organization.

The analysis can also be done at a deeper level. For example, if the purchasing process had turned out to have a high level of risk, purchasing itself could be broken down into more detailed processes, such as Supplier Selection, Issuing Orders to Suppliers, and Monitoring Supplier Performance.

The analysis would need to be occasionally revised, especially if there are significant changes in the industry, business, products/services, processes, and so on.

Approach #2—Consider the Potential Impact of Changes

It's well known that things are more likely to go wrong when changes are made to a system. For example, when a power plant has a scheduled shut down (for example, for maintenance), there is a high probability that there will be an unscheduled interruption within 30 days of bringing it back online.

This approach then says that an audit should be considered after the introduction of something new or changes to existing:

- Products (for example, a new product or an engineering design change)

- Processes (new process, or changes in procedures, personnel, equipment, software, and so on within an existing process)

- Suppliers (for example, a new supplier for an item already provided by a different company)

- The facility (for example, changes in layout, environmental controls)

- Organizational/process objectives and/or metrics

- Management personnel (for example, C-level or process owners) or organizational structure and/or strategy

The potential negative impacts that might be related to these changes should be considered, and an audit plan developed based on what risks might be most relevant. This means the audit program manager needs to be notified of changes that occur, and/or when planning an audit, the degree of change within the audit area is assessed to help focus on any special risks if relevant. Not all changes will be significant enough to warrant an audit, and even if one is warranted, the timing might be delayed if deemed less potentially critical.

Approach #3—Take Feedback on the QMS into Account

There are many sources of feedback for the QMS, and any negative changes in these factors may indicate a need for an audit. Use of performance feedback can be done as part of each audit simply by looking at data related to the process, such as how often customer complaints have led back to the process as the source. How many nonconformities were found during previous audits of the process? How do performance metrics related to the process objectives indicate things are going? The answer to these questions can help an auditor decide whether to increase or decrease the audit depth and/or what aspects of the process to focus on most.

Another way to get feedback is from the management review process. Since the function of management review is to look at how well the QMS is performing, and deciding what actions might be useful or necessary, an output of management review could be adjustments of the audit process.

Should RBQAs be Separate or Integrated?

Risk-based quality audits (RBQAs) could be conducted as separate audits by transferring critical risks to a QMS risk register used to guide these special audits that focus specifically on those processes or process components having higher risk. Or, RBQAs can be integrated into each audit, making it more transparent.

It's also useful to see what other risk-based assessment processes are used within the organization, such as a formal enterprise risk management (ERM) process or the use of risk-based auditing of other management systems such as safety, environmental, and so on. There may be opportunities for sharing of methods for assessing risk and planning and reporting audit results across management systems.

USING ANALYTICS IN THE AUDIT PROCESS

Analytics means different things to different people/organizations, but in general, the terms *data mining, big data, business intelligence*, and *predictive analytics* are all almost synonyms for the use of data and computer software to help make better decisions. For example, Marketing wants to know which potential customers are more valuable so their efforts get higher rewards. Finance wants to know who (or not) to loan money to. Human resources would like to be able to make better hiring decisions. Supply chain personnel would like to be able to respond quicker to disruptions.

Quality auditors would like to know which processes are more appropriate to audit now, as opposed to those that are likely operating well. Think about the 80/20 rule, which would indicate 80 percent of quality problems are likely caused by 20 percent of the processes. But how does one figure out the 20 percent?

In the previous section, the use of a qualitative risk assessment table was presented as one way to identify which processes were more at risk. But that's not the same as having quantitative indicators that indicate that a specific process should be audited. Through the use of analytics, processes can be monitored to detect variances that might be worth exploring deeper with traditional audit techniques.

Of course, some of this is being done by process personnel through the use of process metrics and statistical process control (SPC). In some applications, this is even automated, with alerts provided when special attention is warranted. Auditors can look at these same indicators during audits in order to identify controls to be reviewed and/or audit trails to follow.

However, analytics often involves digging deeper into metrics, especially combinations of metrics, to identify relationships and patterns that might provide greater knowledge of what drives process performance, or whether there are unusual signals. The analytical methods can be very complex, or simple applications such as distribution analysis, clustering, ratios, or correlation. In financial auditing, one of the simplest such techniques involves the use of Benford's Law, which uses distribution analysis.

Benford's Law states that within a set of large numbers, the first digit is more likely (about 30 percent of the time) to be a "1" versus any other digit. The digit "2" is the next highest probability (approximately 18 percent), and so on through the remainder of digits. Now imagine that someone in an organization decides to commit fraud by setting up a fake company as a supplier, and issues purchase orders to that company.

It's quite likely that the "random" dollar amounts they use in the invoices will not follow the distribution one would expect. A financial auditor who uses Benford's Law to analyze invoices might therefore detect that this particular supplier should receive greater attention during the audit (see Figure 5.3). This decision would be based on the difference between the number "expected" based on Benford's law versus "actual." A chi-square analysis could also be used to determine whether the difference is statistically significant.

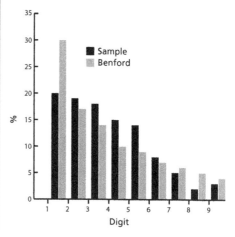

Digit	Number	%	Benford
1	60	20.20%	30.10%
2	57	19.19%	17.61%
3	55	18.52%	12.49%
4	39	13.13%	9.69%
5	36	12.12%	7.92%
6	22	7.41%	6.69%
7	15	5.05%	5.80%
8	6	2.02%	5.12%
9	7	2.36%	4.48%
	297	100.00%	99.90%

Distribution of First Digit In Invoices

Figure 5.3 Use of Benford's Law.

Other examples of use of analytics during financial/GRC (governance, risk, compliance) audits are:

- General ledger – Looking for duplicate entries or unauthorized users
- Purchase-to-pay cycle – Purchase order date is after the date of the invoice, invoice sequence #s
- Payroll – Employee status, hours worked vs. allowed
- P-cards – Split purchases, weekend transactions
- Order-to-cash – Credit limit vs. order sizes, delivery vs. order quantity

In summary, the use of analytics allows these auditors to identify which specific processes and transactions data indicate might be worth looking at during an audit, rather than using a random sample selection. This is basically the use of risk indicators to help focus audit resources. It also means that when a physical audit is performed, it can be done at greater depth.

So how might this apply to quality audits? There are many data generating activities within a QMS, such as:

- Performance data (inspection/test, metrics)
- Calibrations performed (when, results)
- Nonconforming material (quantity, type, cause)
- Supplier performance ratings
- Training records (who, what, when)

Here are a couple of examples of analytics applied to QMS process data:

- **Analysis of Calibration Actions.** An organization has many measurement devices that require calibration quarterly. In order to balance the workload, they do approximately one-third of them each month within a quarter. An analysis of the typical minimum and maximum number calibrated each month of the quarter (when all is well) could be developed, and data for future quarters compared to those norms. Figure 5.4 shows such an analysis and indicates that in the second quarter the number was lower than normal, and in the third quarter it was higher. What does this mean? Perhaps it means some techs were on vacation the second month and they doubled their efforts in the third to make up the schedule. Or maybe the data are fake for the third month, and devices were not actually calibrated but the database was simply updated to indicate they had been.

- **Analysis of Equipment Maintenance.** Figure 5.5 shows a graph of the ratio of the output of a machine (for example, number of parts) to the number of preventive maintenance hours over several months. Note that in the last three to four months, the ratio has increased significantly. Does this mean that preventive maintenance is not being done since production demands have gone up? Is the ratio still within the allowable window that will not impact reliability of the equipment? Has quality of the output of the machine been impacted by the change in the ratio?

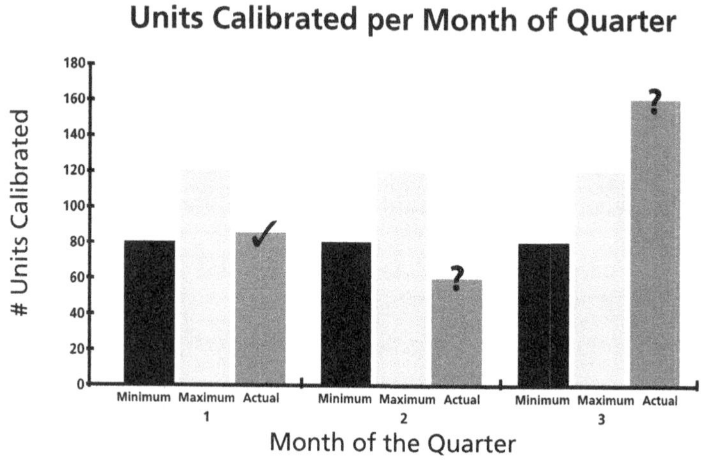

Units Calibrated per Month of Quarter

Figure 5.4 Use of analytics for calibration frequency.

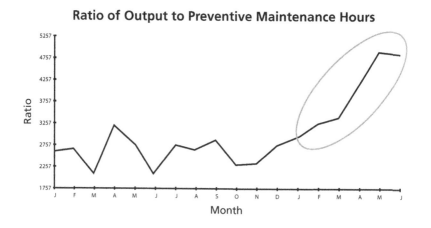

Figure 5.5 Comparing machine output and maintenance hours.

So in these two cases, the auditors are able to determine in advance whether or not they want to perform a physical audit of the calibration and maintenance processes. Some other potential quality audit analytics examples might include:

- **Purchasing:** Ratio of purchases from multiple suppliers of the same part

- **Organization knowledge:** Number of qualified persons per skill area over time

- **Document control:** Date of process change vs. date of training record

- **Complaints:** Complaints vs. experience of sales, shipping, and so on

If a quality audit program manager decides to apply analytics, it's probably best to try a pilot study first. Select a single application, then collect and analyze some baseline data first. Then at a later point in time, repeat the analysis and investigate and/or report any anomalies. Then, simply rinse and repeat. Another option is to identify a quality problem that has previously occurred and see whether analytics might have been able to detect it sooner.

Certain difficulties may be encountered in trying to use analytics. The first is just getting access to the data, such as gaining permission and having it extracted from the source. Another is the time and effort often required to clean up the data and prepare them for use (for example, dealing with missing/incorrect data, formatting them). And of course, confidentiality, privacy, and so on need to be considered.

SHIFTING PRIORITIES DUE TO RISK

In chapter 1 it was mentioned that of the two types of errors an auditor could make, Type 2 was preferable. That is, it's better to mistakenly determine that something is not a nonconformity when it actually is than to say something is a nonconformity when it is not (a Type 1 error). This bias likely came about for two reasons: the philosophy of "innocent until found guilty," and understanding that audits already have a negative perspective in people's mind, and writing a NC when there isn't one will simply make things worse.

However, in today's world where many failures of products and organizations have had significant impacts on peoples' health, finances, careers, and so on, the appetite for risk has been reduced, which means the priority of audit errors is likely to shift to where Type 1 is preferred over Type 2. Of course in high-risk industries, it would be considered a lack of due diligence, perhaps even a dereliction of duty, to ignore something that might have a deleterious effect. For example, ignoring a financial error that might cause the stated earnings of an organization to be incorrect could theoretically result in jail time for senior management.

And quality managers have served time for knowingly allowing defective situations to be ignored in the food industry.

This will call for organizations to properly frame the situation in terms of risk. It is better to avoid a problem that doesn't exist than to not avoid one that does, especially when the risk potential is high.

Another shift that will likely occur is an increase in the use of statistical sampling. Many quality audits use convenience sampling and judgment sampling. While the latter might at least help focus on greater risk (in fact the use of analytics could be interpreted as a guide for judgment sampling), there cannot be a great degree of confidence in audit results due to the small sample sizes often used.

AUDITING RISK MANAGEMENT

Risk management, if done properly, is so integrated into how a business operates that for internal quality auditors it might not significantly impact what they do. However, given the importance of risk management in today's world and the myriad of ways it can be implemented, it is incumbent on quality auditors to be familiar with the overall concept and related process.

Regardless of the scope of interest, risk management has four key steps: 1) Identify potential risks, 2) Assess them for level of risk, 3) Decide how each risk will be treated, and 4) Monitor how well the decision at step 3 came out. Treatment options are usually given as accept the risk (for example, do nothing), transfer the risk (for example, buy insurance or otherwise outsource it), reduce the risk (for example, put in place controls that will cause the probability and/or impact to be less), or avoid the risk (for example, don't do that particular activity). These details are well spelled out, along with key principles, in the ISO 31000 risk management standard.

However, this four-step process can be formalized at a minimal level (think risk-based thinking), more firmly as it applies to products, more broadly as it applies to operations, and/or more strategically as applied to the enterprise. Within a QMS this means deciding whether all processes will be assessed for risk or only those related to product/service creation and delivery (those in the section called Operations in ISO 9001:2015), or all processes (as required by ISO 13485 for medical devices). It can be applied to products using tools such as fault tree analysis and a formal risk management program for new products as defined by ISO 14971.

Risk management is also applied operationally in health and safety, information security, and other management systems. Enterprise risk management (ERM) adds in strategic risks such as failure of an acquisition and financial risks such as exchange rates. But again, the same basic four steps are applied.

For application of risk management to QMS processes, a wide range of other tools can be applied, such as brainstorming, a cause and effect diagram, failure mode and effects analysis (FMEA), and Monte Carlo simulation. For high-impact, low-frequency risks where the number of causes is likely to be smaller, a Bow Tie (see Figure 5.6) is often used. The degree of sophistication of the risk management process and tools will be impacted primarily by the industry and the appetite of senior management for risk. ISO 31010 is a worthwhile reference for persons wanting to know more about risk assessment techniques, as it includes 31 different options.

So auditing risk management is no different than auditing any QMS, other than there may be more formalized language and processes utilized in different industries, processes, and/or products. Auditors should simply understand that the purpose of the controls they are auditing is to help reduce risk, and each organization and/or process owner may carry out the identification, analysis, and monitoring of risks differently.

Appendix C provides examples of items that might be considered during an audit of the quality risk management process.

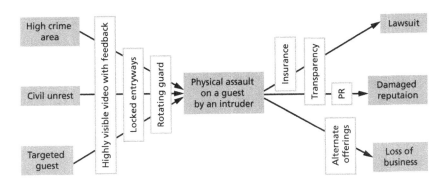

Figure 5.6 Bow tie risk assessment for a hotel.

6

Focus on Governance

Senior management understands audits and the need for them. However, since revenue and profitability are often their major focus, quality audits may not be of high interest. Other types of audits can help get their attention and quality auditors can play a role in these. Even within the quality audit function there can be a lack of attention to purpose, so auditors should step back and review the audit process occasionally to ensure they are remaining vigilant.

STRATEGIC AUDITS

Strategic audits are an evaluation of the progress made toward an organization's strategic objectives by assessing the degree to which the company's strategy is being executed. They don't replace other audits carried out by an organization, but instead supplement them by looking at an aspect of the organization that is often ignored—the organizational change process.

The need for greater attention to strategy implementation was presented by Robert Kaplan and David Norton (of balanced scorecard fame) in an October 2005 *Harvard Business Review* article where they stated that while companies develop strategies, they frequently fail to effectively implement them (that is, turn them into operational processes). The authors' recommendation was to create an office of strategy management, a parallel organization that focuses primarily on strategy development and implementation. Three other authors recommended the creation of a new C-level position titled chief strategy officer (CSO) in the October 2007 issue. The intent of a CSO would be to allow the CEO to focus on keeping current operations running efficiently.

This idea may have merit since the mindsets for tactical (short-term) and strategic (long-term) operations are different. While one is concerned with yesterday's and today's results, the other is concerned with the long term and how well current efforts are moving the organization in that direction. It's difficult to see how a single individual/organizational unit could be responsible for both. Is a separate organization necessary or are there other options? One option might be the use of strategic audits.

Strategic audits don't assess the strategic plan or how it was developed. Instead, they determine the degree to which the strategy has been implemented and executed, including what was done, the resources used to execute it, and the results. Further, they could attempt to determine what issues helped to achieve outstanding results and what might have constrained implementation performance. In essence, if actions, resources, and results are at variance with plans, auditors would try to determine the degree to which organizational systems and/ or cultural factors led to the variance. An added benefit of the strategic audit is that if there is a CSO (whether O is officer or office), the audit will provide an independent assessment of its performance.

Auditors involved in such audits need a broad understanding of business management and excellent communication and analytical skills. In addition, program/project management expertise would be highly valuable, and at least some members of the audit team will likely need specific skills related to technology, finance, and organizational change. Due to the breadth of such audits, auditor independence will likely be problematic, but in an organization philosophically advanced enough to perform strategic audits, this isn't likely to be a barrier.

Perhaps the closest example of a strategic audit is the criteria used to evaluate candidates for the Malcolm Baldrige Performance Excellence Award. The emphasis on executive characteristics such as leadership, strategic planning, and customer focus strongly suggests that someone with the Baldrige assessment experience may be well suited to strategic audits. Someone who has performed only quality, environmental, or safety audits may tend to view things from their specialty area instead of a larger strategic viewpoint.

Strategic audits would begin by first reviewing the strategic plan (likely including interviews of executive committee members), followed by interviews of personnel responsible for implementation along with reviews of processes and records that result from execution of the plan. Strategic audits are likely to be more iterative than most audits since the plan for implementing strategy is not necessarily a rigorously documented process. The key outcomes of the audit should be an improvement in how the organization defines, communicates, and executes strategic change. And as an added benefit, strategic audits can be used to develop high-potential personnel by exposing them to the challenges of executive level operations, decision making, and strategic adaptation.

The idea of strategic audits could also be carried at a less macro level if applied to project management situations. For example, computer software development and Six Sigma projects have a tendency to stretch beyond original target completion dates, and an audit of what was originally planned versus what has actually been accomplished so far could help detect issues that could be addressed sooner and so prevent project failure.

THE FULLY INTEGRATED AUDIT FUNCTION

Integrated audits were discussed in chapter 2. So what is a fully integrated audit function? It is one that pulls together, or at least coordinates, all audits performed within an organization. In addition to the audits done for quality, environment, and safety management systems, others in the organization are auditing financial, information technology, HR compliance, physical security, and perhaps many more. Often there is little to no communication between or across these various functions relative to audit findings, although a good enterprise risk management program will tend to begin this process.

The internal audit function that conducts financial audits is typically overseen by a chief audit executive who reports to the executive audit committee. This reporting structure helps ensure that senior management is aware of significant control weaknesses. But are they aware of weaknesses in the QMS that might put the company at risk?

A fully integrated audit function would create an audit universe that accounts for all processes to be audited and all of the criteria to be applied during those audits. Audits could then be better designed to reduce redundancy and evaluate interconnections between processes and functions. The insight provided by such a holistic view will help ensure that auditors and audit reports are based on a more systemic view of how the organization operates.

ARE YOU GETTING THE FACTS?

Audits will have little value if they are based on bad information. How might that information be inaccurate? Perhaps accidently, but just as likely it may be due to concealment, manipulation, and/or fraud. Policies and procedures may be knowingly ignored, and records intentionally falsified. Auditors may be steered toward or away from certain situations and/or interviewees may simply provide inaccurate information.

So auditors should always be on the lookout for signals that something might be askew. Here are some tell-tail signs:

- The auditor is not allowed free access to items needed to objectively accomplish the audit objective. This might include access to specific locations, equipment, people, products, or records. Another sign might be interviews in which the supervisor or manager insists on answering questions, rather than allowing process personnel to do so.

- Interviewee answers may not address the questions asked or may sound scripted and rehearsed. The interviewee might jump between past/present/future tense for no apparent reason, and speak in generalities (for example, "usually") rather than specifics.

- Body language may indicate an aggressive or defensive mode, such as gaze, hands/arms, or torso. Note that these can be false clues that have nothing to do with the topic itself, but auditors should learn to watch for such signals and adapt their behavior if needed.

- Records may have suspicious similarities such as shared misspellings, using the same phrases, or having been written with the same pen. Electronic records may indicate improper data entry personnel or timing.

- Process variances are acknowledged but explained away as having been a management decision, but there is no documented evidence of a management override. Or the documentation is provided, but overrides are used being used too frequently indicating a problem either with the design of the system or trying to work around it.

So, how should the auditor respond? One option is to simply drill deeper. Increase the sample size, whether it's interviews, product samples, records, and so on. Look for ways to validate the data, regardless of whether they are good or bad. Bracket the problem area by focusing on the preceding and succeeding steps/processes.

Another option is to simply state your concerns and the impact you believe the issues might have on the viability of the audit. A third option is to elevate your concerns to a higher level of the organization. The reaction will perhaps tell you if it is an isolated problem or if management is somehow involved.

If it is a repetitive problem, future audit plans should address them up front. Providing a more specific audit schedule and agenda (including needed samples of personnel, records, and so on) and obtaining senior management written agreement with plan. It may be necessary to delay and reschedule the audit if cooperation and interviewees are not forthcoming as agreed. Document the delay and the reasons, and elevate the information to the management review process.

If all else fails, find an ally and conduct an unannounced audit, perhaps with a management level person acting as co-auditor. Someone from compliance, internal audit, or risk management might also be a good partner.

AVOID THE SLIPPERY SLOPE

The 21st century has so far produced several very visible and expensive examples of management gone wrong and the failure of auditors to uncover and pursue the necessary corrections. Among the earlier ones were the actions at Enron, Adelphia, Tyco, and others that led to the demand for better regulation and the resulting Sarbanes-Oxley Act of 2002. It significantly raised the bar for controls and accountability for financial reporting for public companies.

Unfortunately, laws can't stop auditors determined to protect their interests by ignoring, or not looking for, evidence of fraud. However, it only takes one auditor with high ethical standards to break the case. One such case is documented in *Extraordinary Circumstances: The Journey of a Corporate Whistleblower* by Cynthia Cooper, former vice president of internal audit at WorldCom. It details management's efforts to hide their failing business model by cooking the books.

It's unlikely that any company sets out to create the catastrophes that befall them. What usually happens is that a situation develops that overrides management's better judgment and a decision is made that in hindsight should not have been made. The next step is not admitting the poor decision and correcting course. Instead, management compounds the error with another poor decision and their ride down that slippery slope continues. However, the slide should eventually be detected if auditors do their job.

At WorldCom, the external financial auditing firm (Arthur Anderson) didn't do their job, perhaps because they were at the same time getting huge consulting fees from WorldCom. In essence, they were complicit in the scheme, which also led to the downfall of the audit firm. Fortunately, Cooper (the internal auditor) uncovered the fraud by discovering the phantom profits and complex transaction that generated them.

Such dereliction of duty is not specific to the financial audit world. It could just as well happen in other audit specialties such as quality, environmental, or safety management systems. The ramifications are just as severe, possibly resulting in contract default, product recalls, death or significant injury to customers and/or employees, legal difficulties, loss of market share, and even company failure.

So, what are some of the indicators that might point toward a non-performing audit function?

- **Not focusing on high-risk processes where the likelihood and/or impact of problems is most pronounced.** It doesn't take much effort to identify higher-risk processes in the audit universe prior to developing the annual audit schedule, and then audit those processes more frequently and in greater depth. Ensure that all relevant forms of risk such as regulatory compliance, market risk, and profitability are considered while planning.

- **Trusting but not verifying.** A vital skill for any auditor is critical thinking, so don't accept information at face value. Triangulation, following the trail of the information to original sources, and comparison to the past are some ways to verify data.

- **Allowing management to influence what is documented can weaken an audit.** A typical situation occurs when someone will correct a nonconformity during the audit, and management requests that it not be included in the audit report or that it be downgraded to an observation. This leaves an inaccurate trail. Reports should include exactly what was found, and notes added when useful to clarify how specific situations were addressed.

- **Not following through on corrective actions.** The response to a corrective action needs to be treated with as much attention as was the original audit. Don't accept trivial or incomplete responses. Don't be satisfied with the statement that it was "human error," implying that it was a random and unrepeatable problem. If it was human error and the solution is retraining, ask why the retraining was necessary. For example, what was wrong with the training process when this individual was being trained? Make sure that both physical and systemic causes are addressed unless there is a justifiable reason why such a thorough examination is not necessary.

- **Not looking at the big picture.** A focus exclusively on the immediate problem carries within it the danger of not recognizing the prior problems in the same process. Trend analysis should be done by process, by NC, and by causes, in order to identify patterns that might point to deeper issues.

These issues aren't exclusive to internal auditors, and synergy between them and external auditors can help make the audit process more value added for all parties. This cooperation might include covering areas the other is less able to cover, and providing an independent verification of the other's results.

Several sources of support can help the audit function avoid these danger signs:

- Professional ethics as spelled out by the general audit community and/or professional organizations

- Ensuring that the reporting structure goes all the way to the top of the organization, including the risk management committee, if one exists

- External auditors who audit the internal audit function itself

Section 3
Taking a Broader View
Raising the Bar

7

Cultural and Individual Development

Internal audits affect people and processes. That much is obvious. What is sometimes overlooked is how an audit affects the social aspect of an organization. This comes about not only as a result of how the audit process is designed and the information it produces, but also by the dynamics between auditors and others in the organization.

INTERNAL AUDITS AND ORGANIZATIONAL DEVELOPMENT (OD)

It is estimated that the number of organizations worldwide who have a certified management system for quality, environmental and information security, and so on is now more than 1.5 million. No doubt many have learned the value of implementing formal technical processes for managing the business. However, what many may have missed is the human aspect both during and after certification. This is not unexpected since the technology for managing change (organization development or OD) is not nearly as well known.

OD is the application of behavioral sciences to plan and support organizational strategy and design in order to improve organizational effectiveness. The field integrates theories of psychology, sociology, and anthropology, each of which provides an understanding of how people and organizations work. Different OD "interventions" can be used to move an organization in the desired direction, and may focus on strategic or structural issues (how the organization relates to other entities, how is designed or coordinated), or on more discrete people issues (for example, how effectively individuals or groups plan and/or carry out their work).

Some common OD interventions include:

- **Team Building.** A facilitator interviews members of a work group about their task procedures and presents the information to the group and helps them analyze and plan for improvement. The focus is often on goal setting and whether roles and responsibilities are clearly defined.

- **Survey Feedback.** Members of an organization are surveyed for their feedback on the organization's culture and opinions/ experiences regarding management's leadership, motivation, communication skills, problem-solving ability, rewards programs, and other issues that impact the member's ability to work effectively. Findings are fed back to the organization for their use in defining actions to be taken.

- **Collateral Structures.** A permanent structure or group is set up alongside the formal organizational hierarchy. The group, consisting of members drawn from the formal organization, has the task of working on loosely structured problems that most frequently cross organizational boundaries.

- **Work Redesign.** Jobs are reorganized to give employees more rewarding work. Methods include job rotation, job enlargement (working on a complete process, rather than only part of it), and job enrichment (more responsibility and authority).

This is by no means a full list, as the range of methods used by OD professionals is not only very large but always growing. However, it is interesting to note parallels between the OD role and the audit process. Both evaluate a system by collecting data from that system in order to identify strengths and weaknesses. The data are then fed back to the system in order to develop alternatives that will help it improve.

A core belief of the OD profession is that is the responsibility of personnel within the system to make the decisions, rather than having them imposed on them from the outside. That is, involvement, empowerment, and engagement of employees are core values. Implementation of a QMS can obviously be done from the same viewpoint, using standards/ guidelines as boundaries. While some believe that giving employees such power can create chaos, the design of a QMS has within it a structure for accountability (see Table 7.1) which helps keep processes and people aligned to the organizational objectives.

Table 7.1 Levels of accountability in a QMS.

Level	Process	Purpose
Senior Leadership	Management review	Review system effectiveness
Process owner	Corrective action	Take action to correct problems
Peers	Internal audit	Identify problems
Self	Procedures	Work processes

However, there are also ways the internal audit program can be designed that will impact the degree to which the audit process itself is accepted and how it impacts individuals and work groups. Here are some suggestions:

- The pool of trained auditors should represent as many of the organization's departments and levels as possible. Some organizations use only quality assurance personnel for conducting audits. The weakness in this approach is that they eventually become known as the "audit police" and become seen as detached. A better approach is to design the audit program as a peer review process where all departments participate. Such a diverse pool also helps ensure that independent auditors are available and that no one auditor spends an inordinate portion of time on the process.

- Each department should be asked to nominate members of their department who meet the traits required for effective auditors. The audit pool is more likely to be accepted as trustworthy if employees are asked to nominate members of their own ranks. Additionally, when asking for the nominations, communicating the required traits sends a clear message of the type of people needed in the organization for such an important task, and are in fact, core competencies.

- Membership of the auditor pool and each audit team should be rotated on a regular basis so that each audit can be conducted by a team of auditors selected from the pool. Subsequent audits in the same department or of the same element or process should be conducted by different members of the audit team but perhaps with some overlap. And, the audit pool can itself be changed annually by replacing some auditors with new ones (see Figure 7.1).

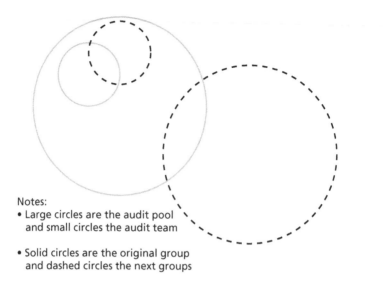

Notes:
• Large circles are the audit pool
  and small circles the audit team

• Solid circles are the original group
  and dashed circles the next groups

Figure 7.1 Rotation of audit pool and audit teams.

The point is that implementing any change in an organization can be viewed as an opportunity to not only change business processes, but also change the culture of the organization. How the implementation is designed and carried out will have a significant impact on whether the change is a positive or negative influence on the culture.

QUALITY AUDITORS AS ROLE MODELS

The third component of an effective audit program beyond its mechanics and its place in the organization is the auditor acting as a quality ambassador. Auditors work to identify weaknesses or opportunities in the quality management system and will influence how others think about both quality and the audit process.

Their influence, of course, comes about as a result of their behavior—how they interact with others. It is known that some behaviors facilitate individual and organizational growth and change, while others can retard it. Here are some simple examples of positive behaviors by auditors:

• Listen to not only what is being said, but also perhaps to what is not being said by an auditee

• Present themselves as being on an equal level with, rather than having positional power over, auditees

- Evaluate compliance with and effectiveness of the management system without allowing personal bias to influence their judgment

- Convince management of the significance of findings while not providing advice on how to correct them

All are essential components of good human interactions that recognize and respect individual roles, responsibilities, and boundaries. For more on human psychology and how it can be applied (or misapplied) during an audit, consider three major theories of psychology: psychoanalytical, behavioral, and humanistic.

The psychoanalytical viewpoint originated by Sigmund Freud states that behavior is a product of one's past and that in order to change, one must discover and resolve issues from the past with which they have not adequately dealt. The behavioral viewpoint (from B.F. Skinner and Ivan Pavlov) states that a person's behavior is a result of external stimuli to which one responds and that by applying the appropriate stimuli, a person can be changed. The humanistic viewpoint (from Carl Rogers and Abraham Maslow) assumes that every individual is on a perpetual journey of personal growth and development and that given a safe environment that supports their effort, people will change in positive ways.

Each of these theories of psychology is correct, given certain circumstances, but none is complete. Rather, it seems that the three of them working together provide a more complete picture of human communication. However, of the three, the humanistic viewpoint is more appropriate in the work environment since it is forward-looking. The psychoanalytical approach is past oriented, and the behavioral view is based on rewards and punishment as motivators.

The humanistic viewpoint itself has several subdivisions, three of which are of interest for their applicability to auditing. They are transactional analysis (TA), the person-centered approach, and Gestalt. Following is a brief description of each along with examples of how they might apply during an audit.

Transactional analysis is a simple way to look at communications patterns between individuals. The premise is that a person has three different ego states that they can use: Parent, Adult, and Child (see Figure 7.2). However, the significance is that the choice of the ego state used in a particular interaction with someone will influence not only how the message will be received but also how the other person responds.

Each of these ego states has both positive and negative aspects. For example, the Parent may provide nurturing to help others become more secure, or can be critical and controlling. The Child may be effective at generating creative ideas or can be rebellious toward authority figures. The Adult can make very rational decisions based on available information, but might not consider the emotional impact on others. What is important is to recognize the ego state being used in a particular situation, and whether it is appropriate.

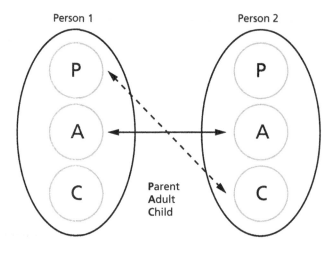

Figure 7.2 Transactional analysis.

For example, consider an audit interview. If the auditor implies that the audit is like a game (child ego state), auditees are not likely to take them seriously, and the perceived value of the audit process will be undermined. If the auditor conducts the interview in a manner that implies that their findings can cause grief for the auditee (parent ego state), then the audit process will be seen as having a negative, rather than positive purpose. This could also occur during a closing meeting, where an auditor may emphasize the importance of his/her role to try to force a manager to accept a nonconformity for which there is not sufficient supporting evidence. The auditor might insist that the interviewee take corrective action in a public way that embarrasses the interviewee. Obviously, auditors should use the adult ego state role, even (or perhaps especially) when the auditees are not using it.

The *person-centered approach* emphasizes that a particular climate, called a "facilitative psychological attitude," is necessary in order for individual change to occur. Three basic conditions are said to be necessary in order for such an environment to exist:

- **Congruence**—People must be genuine and authentic in their relationships with each other

- **Unconditional positive regard**—People are accepted regardless of how their beliefs or customs might differ

- **Empathic understanding**—The ability to understand how another sees a situation

The idea is that a person is more at ease and less defensive when around someone who demonstrates these three attitudes. Viewed from the other side, when people are in a climate that does not value acceptance and understanding, they are likely to use some of their energy in order to protect their sense of self. This same energy could instead be used in more positive ways, such as trying new behaviors that may be more effective.

The person-centered approach is applicable during an audit interview. An auditor can choose to communicate with auditees in a caring, non-judgmental, understanding way, and thereby improve the chances of obtaining complete and accurate information on the status of the management system. Alternatively, auditees could be put on the defensive if given the feeling that it is the person rather than the system that is being audited.

The *Gestalt philosophy* is based on the concept of the difference between "figure" (what we see, hear, think, and/or feel) and "ground" (what we ignore), and focuses on trying to raise awareness of information that may have been ignored. The theory is that greater awareness will allow more options to be seen, resulting in a greater probability of positive change.

In auditing, this means that attention should often be paid to both what auditees are saying and are not saying, what they do and don't do, and what records demonstrate and don't demonstrate. In addition, it is useful for the auditor to be aware of questions they did ask as well as those they felt like asking, but didn't.

Another element of the Gestalt approach is the cycle of experience, which shows stages a person or organization goes through in responding to situations. A simplified version of the cycle has four basic steps (see Figure 7.3): 1) awareness, 2) willingness, 3) movement, and 4) evaluation.

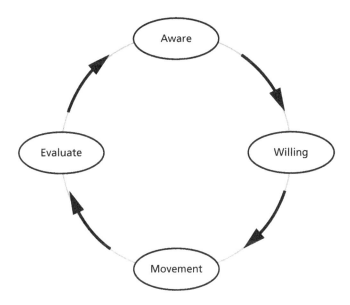

Figure 7.3 Gestalt cycle of change.

Table 7.2 Gestalt cycle during audit interview.

Stage of Cycle	Possible Auditee Issue	Possible Auditor Response
Awareness	Unsure of audit purpose and scope	Confirm that manager has informed them; if not, do so before beginning interview
Willingness	Concerned about work process and possible ramifications of audit findings	Be patient, communicate anonymity of findings if possible
Movement	Does not have sufficient time to answer questions due to conflicting schedule	Communicate understanding and modify audit plan
Evaluation	Need for closure on questions already answered	Summarize findings

Step 1 is defined as the need to first become aware of the situation. Step 2 indicates that even if one is aware, one may or may not be willing to respond. Step 3 implies that even if willing, one may or may not actually make the needed change. Once movement is made, Step 4 provides a review to determine what the impact has been. As with the PDCA cycle, stopping at or leaving out a step of the cycle results in a less than optimum final result. Table 7.2 shows an example of a possible problem at each stage of the cycle of experience that might occur during an audit interview, and how an auditor might consider reacting.

Gestalt also recognizes the desire of any system to remain in a stable state and views resistance to change as a natural defense. That is, individuals and organizations resist change largely due to the instability that it creates. In order to avoid having to change, mechanisms such as deflection, projection, and retroflection are used. Although these defenses help to prevent one from being overwhelmed by external and often conflicting stimuli, when the effect is to prevent one from adapting to reality, the mechanisms use energy that could instead be put into evaluation and change.

An example of resistance in auditing might be an auditee who repeatedly avoids answering an auditor's questions by talking about something different (deflection). The auditor might interpret this resistance as a personal attack, become angry, and threaten the auditee.

However, this is likely to cause more resistance by the auditee. A more positive approach would be to ask the auditee to help determine how the system could be assessed. This approach recognizes that resistance is a natural response and tries to channel it into a direction that may accomplish the mission. It is, of course, important to recognize that sometimes resistance may be due to personal problems that the auditor should not, and is not, qualified to explore.

Auditors are given a position that is considered an important role for the organization and they become very visible through that role. They must, therefore, consider whether they are providing a role model for others that demonstrates behaviors that contribute to effective organizational improvement.

INDIVIDUAL DEVELOPMENT FOR AUDITORS

Development of an organization means a change in capabilities. While some of these capabilities will be due to changes in technology and business models, a large aspect of successful change involves the learning of individual employees. The activities required when auditors are planning, conducting, and reporting audits provide significant learning for some of them. Following are some examples:

- The audit process creates significant opportunities for cross-functional learning. A person working in department A who must review procedures used by department B then evaluate how well these procedures are being followed will learn about activities (other than their own) that are also important to the organization. The tunnel vision that sometimes results when viewing only one's own departmental purpose can be alleviated.

- The audit process requires development of a planning horizon. Some positions in an organization may provide little opportunity to learn how to plan, due to the redundant or short-term nature of the tasks performed by that position. By way of contrast, an individual planning for an audit must think ahead to activities that will be done perhaps one or two weeks later.

- The process develops investigatory and logical skills. The null hypothesis for internal audits is that the system is working. It is the auditor's job to look for evidence that demonstrates that either it is or is not working. The traceability aspects of auditing and the interaction of the various processes that must be audited provide an opportunity for the auditor to learn to think logically and to plan and conduct an evidence verification step for follow-up.

- The process builds persuasive ability. Auditors must be able to present their evidence for any findings during the closing meeting and/or in the final report, and convince the relevant managers that the evidence is not only valid but that it shows a variance from the desired state.

- The process enhances the auditor's ability to maintain role clarity. Individuals trying to initiate a change without having the appropriate authority to do so can be a source of conflict within the organization. Therefore, auditors must be able to remove themselves from their normal position in the organization and take on a special role that has clearly defined boundaries and responsibilities.

- The process helps develop systems-thinking ability. An internal auditor must consider the potential results (outcomes) of an inadequately designed or implemented process even if the process is being done according to the procedures and there are no nonconformities. The exercise helps prepare the auditor for better failure prevention planning in the future, as well as more effective corrective actions.

One of the reasons for the use of audit teams rather than single auditors is that some of these learnings will be minimal for some personnel, while for others it can transform their view of what they are capable of accomplishing. Pairing auditors so that they can learn from each other not only helps the auditees get a better audit but also helps the auditors learn more rapidly.

CHECKING AUDITOR CALIBRATION

One thing that causes grief for many QMS managers is auditors who misinterpret standards or evidence, and write nonconformities based on this misinterpretation or their personal biases. Since auditors are basically collecting data, perhaps the concept of measurement system evaluation should be used to determine how well auditors' minds are calibrated.

One technique that can be used is called Attribute Agreement Analysis, which is basically gage R&R used on attribute data. It is included in Minitab, SigmaXL, and other statistical packages, and if simple percentages are sufficient (as opposed to statistical confidence limits or significance tests), the analysis can be done without them.

Let's begin with a simple situation: There are three internal quality auditors working in the same organization. The quality manager wants to see how effective they are at interpreting audit situations (for example, whether or not a situation is a NC). So the manager created five good scenarios (not NCs) and five bad ones (NCs). The quality manager randomly organizes the situations and has each auditor review them and make a decision as to whether or not each is a NC. Table 7.3 is an example of the results. There are three different views that can be taken of this data.

How well does each auditor agree with the standard? Auditor #1 was correct 80 percent of the time and committed one Type 1 and one Type

Table 7.3 Auditor calibration data.

Auditor	Sample	Response	Standard
1	1	0	0
1	2	0	0
1	3	1	0
1	4	0	0
1	5	0	0
1	6	1	1
1	7	1	1
1	8	0	1
1	9	1	1
1	10	1	1
2	1	1	0
2	2	0	0
2	3	0	0
2	4	0	0
2	5	0	0
2	6	1	1
2	7	1	1
2	8	1	1
2	9	1	1
2	10	1	1
3	1	0	0
3	2	0	0
3	3	0	0
3	4	0	0
3	5	0	0
3	6	1	1
3	7	1	1
3	8	1	1
3	9	1	1
3	10	1	1

Sample = audit situation #

Responses:
0 = auditor determined not a NC
1 = auditor classified it a NC

Standard = what correct answer should be
0 = situation is not a NC
1 = situation is a NC

2 error. Auditor #2 was correct 90 percent of the time but committed one Type 1 error. Auditor #3 was correct 100 percent of the time. The Fleiss's Kappa statistic indicates that Auditor #1 needs to be calibrated (kappa = .6), while Auditors 2 and 3 are considered acceptable (based on a Kappa of approximately .8 for Auditor 2 and 1.0 for Auditor 2); Minitab indicates that Kappa less than .7 indicates a need to improve the measurement system, while if it is .9 it is considered excellent. Of course, there could be a problem with the standards themselves.

How well do the auditors agree with each other? The auditors only agreed with each other 70% of the time, with a Kappa of .6. This indicates a lack of agreement that should be addressed. Perhaps getting Auditor #1 better calibrated would suffice.

How well do all auditors as an aggregate agree with the standard? Of the 10 samples, seven (70 percent) were properly labeled. The Fleiss' Kappa statistic is again approximately .8, which would be considered acceptable.

How well does each auditor agree with his/her self? This cannot be done since each auditor evaluated each situation only one time. Having them reevaluate each situation would likely not be considered an independent sample since having seen it before might impact their analysis. This could perhaps be overcome by having a larger set of sample situations and allowing a sufficient amount of time between the evaluations.

So in summary, although the overall system appears to be acceptable, perhaps some work should be done to help Auditor#1 perform better. Depending on the type of organization (for example, degree of risk of incorrect audit decisions) perhaps a higher level of performance is desired. The analysis could also delve deeper into the specific types of errors in order to make this decision as well as to help develop better auditor training criteria.

Note: A sample size of 50 is often recommended for attribute studies, but these studies usually involve testing both physical (for example, eyesight) and cognitive aspects of the persons being studied. In the case of audits it is purely a cognitive test, so an organization may decide to use fewer than 50 and only accept a Kappa of 1.0.

WHERE DO INTERNAL AUDITORS GO NEXT?

Individuals are ultimately responsible for managing their own careers. On the other hand, organizations have a vested interest in maintaining an adequate pool of skills that are necessary to conduct business while simultaneously looking at who is developing in line with future needs.

One of the development opportunities for many jobs is to be an auditor. As stated earlier, auditors either have or typically develop critical thinking skills, a systems perspective, and the ability to communicate effectively. In addition, auditors are exposed to many business processes in which they themselves have never worked.

So a fundamental question should be, "Where do the individuals who have taken on the role of quality auditor eventually end up in the organization?" Do they gain knowledge from the experience that allows them to take on broader or deeper roles, or do they simply return to where they were? One would hope that being an auditor provides a growth experience that helps individuals develop career-wise. And that might even include moving into the internal (financial) audit function.

One client organization used whether or not someone had been an internal auditor as a factor when deciding if someone was a viable candidate for a position in supervisory/management-type roles. The assumption was that not only would they know more about how the business operated (outside their current function) but also that they had demonstrated the ability to think strategically and analytically, and willingness to go beyond their own job duties.

So while there's no one right answer to the question of where auditors go, there are likely some wrong ones. If they do not develop as a result of the auditing experience, then either the individual has limited interests or capabilities, the audit program is not well designed and executed so as to ensure development of skills, or the organization doesn't recognize the potential for this pool of experienced personnel.

After all, effective auditors must be logical in their thinking and have the ability to collect and analyze data. They have to be able to do this related to how well processes are achieving objectives. What job in an organization wouldn't benefit from someone with such skills?

8

Quality Auditing in the Future

There's no doubt that auditing will be with us for the foreseeable future. The Institute of Internal (financial) Auditors has more than 170,000 members, with more than 100,000 of those being certified. There are more than 30,000 ASQ Certified Quality Auditors. And, of course, many internal auditors have no formal auditor recognition outside their organization. But the product and organizational failures that have occurred and vulnerability of business systems to disruption from many sources indicate that there is always a need for vigilance performed not only by process owners but also by independent audit personnel.

The question, though, is how will auditing change? This chapter will look at the question from several perspectives. Many of the ideas have been under discussion within a small portion of the profession for some time, but have yet to become mainstream. Since they aren't fully utilized, the information available on exactly what to do and how is limited, so these pieces are brief. It is hoped readers will find some worthwhile of consideration for their organizations.

APPRECIATE (INQUIRY) AUDITS

Before training internal auditors for companies the author was helping implement ISO 9001, a session was often held with the executive team to help create the right mindset, such as understanding that auditors are "evaluating the system, not people." The session was usually started by asking the question, "When I mention the word *audit*, what other words come to mind?" Their answers would be recorded on a flip chart and always included "IRS."

The event that indicated that such an overview might be of value was during an auditor training course when personnel from two departments—quality, and production—would not talk to each other (who would have thought)! It seems the company had been performing internal quality audits for a while, but obviously not from a healthy perspective.

Auditing has probably always had a negative connotation, and any effort auditors can take to help alleviate people's concerns is likely to be well spent. In this regard, one of the intervention techniques from the field of OD, appreciative inquiry (AI), has been adapted to quality audits by some organizations.

AI has the philosophy that rather than looking for what is not working (seen as a negative view) in an organization or process, it's best to look for what is working in order to create a more positive experience. When applied to audits, the findings are more likely to be documented as opportunities for improvement, rather than NCs, although the audits can of course also identify NCs.

Questions during an appreciate audit are more likely to ask about how success was achieved in a specific situation, or how auditees would ensure a successful outcome. Similar to a process approach to auditing, suppliers and customers of the process will be included in the audit, but as validators of information provided by process owners. Reviews of records are not done during the audit interviews since it is the conversation (their "stories") that is the objective.

Appreciate audits are perhaps especially useful in organizations where the system is mature, meaning there are fewer NCs, so audits can then focus on identifying best practices and improvement opportunities. Such audits would also likely be more appreciated (no pun!) in organizations performing social-type work than technical-type work, due to the difference in perspectives of "problems."

An audit had been performed of the maintenance process and feedback given to the plant manager. His response was, "You just called my baby ugly." Perhaps an appreciate approach would have been useful here, asking questions such as, "What are you most proud of regarding the maintenance process?" and "Where do you believe there are some opportunities to make it better?"

AUTOMATED CONTINUOUS AUDITING

A 1999 study by the author looked at how much changes in politics, economics, social ideology, and technology impacted our world. The conclusion was that technology ultimately drives everything in an open society. That is, as technology changes, our social, economic, and political worlds adapt.

The same is obviously true for auditing. As demonstrated in chapter 2, technology has made virtual audits a lot easier, more viable, and accepted. In chapter 5 the power of computer technology to analyze data to help point out where audits might be more valuable was demonstrated. These two in combination with digital business process management systems (BPMS) will have dramatic effects on auditing.

Remember that management system audits are simply another form of inspection, but one that's conducted at the process or system level rather than on a product. And those audits use sampling rather than evaluating 100 percent of the cases. But with automated continuous auditing, every transaction that occurs within a computer can be tested for compliance. This means the logic of auditing can be built into the BPMS (planning the audit), and someone will need to respond (conducting the audit) when the software issues an alert.

Here are some examples of continuous auditing that might be applied to a QMS:

- If someone performs a test and that person is required to provide traceability back to the test device by entering a serial number, have the system automatically search the calibration database to determine whether the device is within its calibration window

- If a piece of equipment (again, perhaps a serial number) is entered into a production record for something that is being produced, have the system search the maintenance database to make sure it's within its maintenance period

- When someone enters the supplier ID and/or batch # for raw materials about to be used, have the system check to make sure the supplier is still considered qualified and/or that the batch # has actually been approved/released for use

- If a computer user is using a particular application, have the system check to make sure that individual (for example, based on their sign in to the system) is qualified to do that job by checking the training database

- If someone performs an audit have the system check to make sure they are independent of the area to be audited

Note that these do not preclude conducting random physical audits of these processes, but by having the system automatically checking each transaction and issuing warnings when there are outliers, auditor time is likely to be better spent. However, there will often be significant effort required to build the logic into the computer systems.

For someone interested in trying automated continuous audits, it begins with identifying data sources that are computerized that auditors would typically be tracing back to during an audit. Then look for where this information would be valuable as part of a process check and automate that check.

Since we're discussing computers, how about Technology Enhanced Interviews? Ok, this one's going to push the limits a bit. But technology enabled with artificial intelligence will no doubt one day be able to read the face of the person being audited and detect whether or not the person is lying, avoiding the truth, or other deceptive behaviors. Suppose you could get an app for your phone that uses the camera for this!

CASE MANAGEMENT AUDITS

Much of the auditing literature is focused on auditing repetitive business processes. But some organizations don't have repetitive processes since each customer wants something different. That doesn't mean there aren't some repetitive processes that will be used, but the chain from order receipt through order delivery cannot be predicted until the customers have made known their requirements.

An example is an individual who shows up at a hospital ER. The clerk will go through a standard process (what's wrong, do you have insurance, let me see ID, and so on). For most people, the next step will be to see an ER doctor. But where they go from there will depend on how the specific condition. Their next step might be the OR, radiology, pharmacy, hospital, home, or even the morgue!

Organizations that manage retirement benefits are similar. The benefits available to one employee might be significantly different from another due to when the employee worked for the company, choices that employee made when selecting from benefit options, and so on. Audits of different transactions can require looking at significantly different processes, using conditional thinking all along the path. This is quite different from auditing where every customer order follows the same standard path and has the same, or at least highly similar, basic requirements.

Case audits are more similar to project management audits. What was originally planned may need to change based on the results of previous steps, customer change requests, and/or resource availability. Such audits call for much greater auditor flexibility, rather than just going in with a standard set of questions to check off.

BUSINESS AUDITS

Peter Drucker first mentioned the idea of business audits in his 1993 book titled *Post-Capitalist Society*. The number of times that companies have gone under or have announced major layoffs since the 1980s indicates it may be well past time. The purpose of business audits is to hold senior executives accountable for effective management of society's resources. Looking at profitability is far too late and too narrowly focused, and of course, the financial books can easily be manipulated.

You do know there are two sets of books, right? One for the IRS that shows low profits, with resulting minimal tax payments, and one for stockholders showing high profitability, so they'll buy more stock…and these are both legal. But of course there may also be a third!

Business audits are obviously difficult to perform. The process requires knowledge of the industry, of finance, of strategy formulation, of operations management, and so on. The ideal audit team would represent customers, suppliers, shareholders, employees, and general society, and would ensure that the business is being managed according to generally accepted effective business principles, and perhaps even more importantly, is able to innovate.

While business audits might be seen as similar to strategic audits, there is one major difference. Strategic audits do not look at whether or not the strategy is a good one, but instead how well it was carried out. But business audits would also assess the viability of the organization's strategy, and would perhaps be organized by industry associations.

What does this have to do with quality audits? Remember that the quality system is about ensuring that customers get what they want when they want it, so the QMS is the core business process. This means all the other processes are there in order to support the quality system. Think total quality management or quality of how the entire business is managed.

CULTURE AUDITS

In risk management, the Three Lines of Defense model is often used to emphasize the levels of risk controls in an organization. The first line is made up of the process controls that have been put in place and the process owners responsible for managing them; the second line consists of the internal control and compliance functions (of which QA would be one) who provide guidance for controls design and implementation; and the third line is independent assurance (internal audit). This author has many times stated that the fourth line is organizational culture (maybe it should be the first!).

In 2016 the Institute of Internal Auditors published *Global Perspective and Insight: Auditing Culture—A Hard Look at the Soft Stuff*. In it they discuss issues that could be considered during an audit that are indicators of culture, such as how often the company shows up negatively in the news, how much time they have to spend in the courtroom defending their business practices, and the perception of employees of the importance of following policies and procedures and for reporting misconduct.

Internal quality auditors are not likely to be asked to conduct an audit of the culture, but as part of conducting audits, they certainly have opportunities to hear and observe things that could give rise to systemic negative cultural issues. At a minimum, auditors should ensure that any information that might indicate culture problems is shared through appropriate channels.

AUDITOR SKILLS AND ETHICS

Greed, ethics, fraud. Unfortunately these are harder to detect through audits than simple process deviations. Until that phone app for detecting liars that was mentioned earlier is available, it probably won't get any easier. Perhaps the best auditors can do is make sure they have the appropriate skills for any audit they perform and apply professional ethics.

The skill set of quality auditors is likely to change based on the way business processes are changing. Not only do we have BPMS, but auditors are increasingly likely to run into more sensors, robots, the cloud, and other technologies. Knowledge of software engineering and software auditing will likely be highly beneficial.

A business mindset has always been useful but is perhaps even more important today. The introduction of risk management in QMS standards has put something on the plate that senior management is highly interested in, and evaluating risk management can't be done very effectively if one isn't aware of how business strategy is developed and the links to enterprise risk management.

On the behavioral side, auditors need to not only be aware of ethical principles and practices as they apply to auditing but also whether or not they have the wherewithal to draw the line at the appropriate point, regardless of the consequences. It's well known that whistleblowers typically suffer immensely even though their actions were appropriate.

The author was highly impressed a few years ago when a quality engineer described a situation where a plant manager asked him to sign off on defective parts and indicated if he didn't, he would be fired. The QE didn't sign off and did lose his job. That can be very hard for someone to do when he or she has a mortgage, children, and so on.

However, each person is morally obligated to carry out the agreed duties. Auditors are there to report requirements compliance and nonconformances. Not doing so is a professional and ethical lapse that reflects poorly on self, the audit profession, the company, and society. If someone is not willing to do so, he or she should decline to be an auditor.

SUMMARY

This book has focused on one goal: to present many different views of quality audits and how they can contribute to organizations. Every organization is in a different place in its life cycle, and every audit program likewise. However, as with any field, there is a need to be continually looking for ways to add greater value and improve efficiency.

The primary role of auditing is one of governance. How QMS audits can contribute to that needs to be a frequent topic of conversation between quality and senior management, with resulting audit program objectives being defined and measured. At a minimum two questions should be asked: 1) Is there an internal quality audit program strategy and related objectives, and 2) Does it link to the organization's strategic direction and key risks? The concept of a balanced scorecard might also be of value, measuring the impact of the program control effectiveness, auditor development, culture, and so on.

One way of evaluating an audit program is through the use of a maturity matrix. Table 8.1 is one such matrix. Note that reaching levels 2 or 3 does not mean giving up what one was doing at the lower levels, but instead mixing/blending as needed for each specific audit purpose.

In closing, it is my firm belief that while audits can add value, they don't necessarily do so in many cases. It is hoped that this book will help the reader not only determine the value being delivered, but also find ways to increase that value.

Table 8.1 Audit maturity matrix.

Area to Assess	Level 1	Level 2	Level 3
Focus of audits	Compliance only	Risks & performance	Improvement opportunities
Frequency of audits	Infrequent (e.g., annually)	Frequent (e.g., monthly)	Continuous (layered audits and/or computerized monitoring)
Auditors	Most by a single auditor	Several, but primarily from department responsible for system (e.g., QA for QMS)	Cross-functional, including members of multiple departments and levels
Organizational view of audits	Negative	Accepting	Positive learning process
Integration of audits	One management system at a time	Multiple systems but separate from GRC	Fully integrated and reporting to CAE
Use of metrics	Track number of NCs and response time	Audit effectiveness and efficiency	Trends in organizational metrics used to drive audits, as well as measure their long-term effects

Appendix A
Example Audit Situations

Following are examples of relatively simple situations the author often sprinkles throughout internal quality audit training courses. They make for short but lively discussions that help trainees think about boundaries, nonconformities, and acceptable audit practices.

Following are some audit situations. What would you do?

1. You show up for the opening meeting at the scheduled time, and a key manager isn't there.

2. As you begin the audit, using a checklist that was prepared from the auditee quality manual/procedures, you learn that the issue of the documentation you used was out of date.

3. You find two copies of the same specification (same revision number and date), but some of the information contained in the two copies is different.

4. You are observing an operator testing a part, and the part shows to be out of spec. The operator re-masters the gage and rechecks the part, and it is in spec.

5. Two operators are using identical machines and making the same part number. They're using different methods to load the part into the machine, and one operator is checking parts against the spec twice as often as the other operator.

6. The shipping log shows that order #10756 was shipped on September 12. The contract specified a ship date of September 10.

7. You ask the receiving inspection supervisor how often he pulls samples from incoming goods. He states that it depends on how badly the parts are needed by production. The quality manual says lots are to be sampled every fifth receival for each part number.

8. The tensile strength tester in the test lab has no sticker showing the last/next date of calibration.

9. You've asked for supplier approval records for two specific suppliers and were told by the purchasing agent that they are in long-term storage only, which is in a warehouse several miles away.

10. You ask the maintenance manager about the company's quality policy. He states that it is just a piece of paper to show the customer, and doesn't mean anything.

11. The human resources manager gives you four employee training files so you can check training records. One of the employees did not attend the required SPC course.

12. An operator is cleaning his work area and moves a box of scrap materials away from a corner. You notice that the electrical cable running up the wall has been crushed, and some of the insulation stripped away.

13. In reviewing nonconforming material reports, you find one part number has been written up six times over the last year for the same failure. Corrective action was indicated to have been taken, and signed off, each time.

14. The operator has been maintaining a control chart, which has gone out of control several times. None of the points out of control is circled on the chart.

15. A box of material has been tagged "Reject." It is sitting next to several other boxes of "Accept" parts.

16. The heat treat process operator is on vacation this week, and the supervisor indicates that he transferred a good operator from the machining department to cover during the week.

17. A few weeks ago you sent an audit report to the manager of a department you audited. In the report, you asked for some evidence that was to be forthcoming from the audit. You also called the manager just a few days ago to remind her of the request, but she seemed unresponsive.

18. You were requested by the Quality Manager to audit an area that you weren't really comfortable with due to the technical nature of the processes to be audited. You agreed when the quality manager said you could call him during the audit and ask about any areas where you were uncertain. You're now in the middle of the audit and called the quality manager to get clarification about how to apply an external specification to your product. The explanation the quality manager gave you doesn't sound logical, but he insists it's appropriate. If what you believe to be the case is true, it means that nonconforming product is being shipped to customers.

19. You sent out the audit report last week. As you were filling your audit notes away today, you noticed that you'd left an audit finding (nonconformity) out of the audit report.

20. You're interviewing a Product Engineer. Rather than answering your questions, each time you ask something he instead goes off on some rampage about the quality system, the documentation required, or how the organization treats engineers. You've been at it now for 30 minutes, and still don't know if he understands his responsibilities in the system.

21. Since the last audit, you conducted the company has installed a new product (and related production processes) in the plant. They aren't included in the quality manual and aren't mentioned in the scope on their certificate of quality system registration.

22. As you conduct the audit, every time you go into a different department, your escort is handed money.

23. You're running behind the schedule you'd set up for today's audit. The manager of the department you're auditing says, "Let's go out to lunch. I can answer a lot of your questions then. I'll buy."

24. At the closing meeting, a manager disagrees with a nonconformity found in her department, even though she'd indicated agreement earlier in the day when you found it. Her department is the only one who had any nonconformities, and she doesn't appear to want to be singled out as failing at her job.

25. You've found a nonconformity. However, the Quality Manager says that the registrar also tried to write it up during the last surveillance audit, but the manager was able to convince them it wasn't actually a violation of the quality system standard.

Appendix B
SIPOC Form for Audit Planning

Process Name:				
Suppliers	Inputs	Process	Outputs	Customers
	Input Metrics		Output Metrics	
Process Resources & Controls				
Equipment:				
Information:				
People:				

Appendix C
Quality Risk Management Audit Questions

Following are some example questions used to teach auditors to audit quality risk management applications:

- Is there a defined process for risk assessment?
- Does it indicate where/when/how the assessment should be carried out?
- Does it indicate what levels of action could be taken based on assessment findings?
- Are personnel who perform assessments properly qualified?
- Does the process include consideration of skills, equipment, and so on capacity/capability?
- Does it take into account past performance and/or company or industry benchmarks?
- Was action taken for each item that required action?
- Is there justification for actions that were (and were not) taken?
- Would a rational person agree with the justification?
- Did the mitigation plan bring the risk to acceptable levels?
- For each identified risk, have there been failures that exceeded the defined expectations for:
  o Frequency
  o Impact
  o Controls
- When a risk event occurs, is it reported to appropriate levels of management?
- Is there evidence that management reviews to determine whether additional action is necessary?

Recommended Reading

Asbury, Stephen. *Health and Safety, Environmental and Quality Audits: A Risk-Based Approach*, 2nd ed. New York: Routledge, 2014.

Beitel, Ardith. "Transitional Auditing—Navigating Through the Chaos," *The Journal for Quality & Participation* (January 2017).

Coleman, Lance. *Advanced Quality Auditing: An Auditor's Review of Risk Management, Lean Improvement, and Data Analysis*. Milwaukee: ASQ Quality Press, 2015.

Griffiths, Phil. *Risk-Based Auditing*. New York: Routledge, 2005.

ISO 19011. *Guidelines for Auditing Management Systems*, 2011.

Jacka, Mike. "Internal Audit Jokes.," https://iaonline.theiia.org/internal-audit-jokes

Livingston, Peter. "The Best Audit Ever," http://www.guardianonline.co.nz/schools/the-best-audit-ever/

Marks, Norman. *World Class Internal Audit: Tales from My Journey*. CreateSpace, 2014.

Morris, Jon. "Smooth Approach: Taking the Turbulence out of the Audit Process with a New System.," *Quality Progress* (October 2008): 34–41.

Pfannerstill, Robert. *The Progressive Audit: A Toolkit for Improving Your Organizational Quality Culture*. Milwaukee: ASQ Quality Press, 2005.

Russell, J.P. (ed.).*The ASQ Auditing Handbook, Fourth Edition*. Milwaukee: ASQ Quality Press, 2012.

Russell, J.P., and Shauna Wilson., *eAuditing Fundamentals: Virtual Communication and Remove Auditing*. Milwaukee: ASQ Quality Press, 2013.

Smith, J.B. *The Art of Integrating Strategic Planning, Process Metrics, Risk Mitigation, and Auditing*. Milwaukee: ASQ Quality Press, 2016.

Index

WHY ASQ?

ASQ is a global community of people passionate about quality, who use the tools, their ideas and expertise to make our world work better. ASQ: The Global Voice of Quality.

FOR INDIVIDUALS

Advance your career to the next level of excellence.

ASQ offers you access to the tools, techniques and insights that can help distinguish an ordinary career from an extraordinary one.

FOR ORGANIZATIONS

Your culture of quality begins here.

ASQ organizational membership provides the invaluable resources you need to concentrate on product, service and experiential quality and continuous improvement for powerful top-line and bottom-line results.

www.asq.org/why-asq

ASQ
The Global Voice of Quality

Sidebar labels: TRAINING · CERTIFICATION · CONFERENCES · MEMBERSHIP · PUBLICATIONS

BELONG TO THE
QUALITY COMMUNITY

JOINING THE ASQ GLOBAL QUALITY COMMUNITY
GIVES YOU A STRONG COMPETITIVE ADVANTAGE.

For people passionate about improvement, ASQ is the global knowledge network that links the best ideas, tools, and experts — because ASQ has the reputation and reach to bring together the diverse quality and continuous improvement champions who are transforming our world.

- 75,000 individual and organizational members in 150 countries
- 250 sections and local member communities
- 25 forums and divisions covering industries and topics
- 30,000+ Quality Resources items, including articles, case studies, research and more
- 19 certifications
- 200+ training courses

ASQ
The Global Voice of Quality

For more information, **visit asq.org/communities-networking.**

ASQ'S
ONLINE
QUALITY
RESOURCES
IS THE
PLACE TO:

- Stay on top of the latest in quality with Editor's Pick and Most Popular

- Browse topics in Learn About Quality

- Find definitions in the Quality Glossary

- Search ASQ's collection of articles, books, tools, training, and more

QUALITY RESOURCES
www.asq.org/quality-resources

Connect with ASQ staff for personalized help hunting down the knowledge you need, the networking opportunities that will keep your career and organization moving forward, and the publishing opportunities that offer the best fit for you.

www.asq.org/quality-resources

ASQ
The Global Voice of Quality

TRAINING   CERTIFICATION   CONFERENCES   MEMBERSHIP   PUBLICATIONS

ASK A LIBRARIAN

Did you know?

Quality Resource contains a wealth of knowledge and information available to ASQ members and non-members.

A librarian is available to answer research requests using ASQ's ever-expanding library of relevant, credible quality resources, including journals, conference proceedings, case studies and Quality Press publications.

ASQ members receive free internal information searches and reduced rates for article purchases.

You can also contact the Quality Information Center to request permission to reuse or reprint ASQ copyrighted material, including journal articles and book excerpts.

For more information or to submit a question, visit asq.org/quality-resources.

ASQ
The Global Voice of Quality™

TRAINING   CERTIFICATION   CONFERENCES   MEMBERSHIP   PUBLICATIONS